STEP-BY-STEP

COMPLETE
Indian
COOKING

D0492675

STEP-BY-STEP

COMPLETE

Indian

COOKING

CARA HOBDAY

LOUISE STEELE

First published in Great Britain in 1995 by
Parragon
Unit 13–17
Avonbridge Trading Estate
Atlantic Road
Avonmouth
Bristol BS11 9QD

Copyright © Parragon 1995

Reprinted in 1997

ISBN 0-7525-0126-7

Produced by Haldane Mason, London

Printed in Italy

Acknowledgements:
Art Direction: Ron Samuels
Editor: Vicky Hanson
Series Design: Pedro & Frances Prá-Lopez/Kingfisher Design
Page Design: Somewhere Creative
Photography: Iain Bagwell, Martin Brigdale, Amanda Heywood, Joff Lee
Styling: Rachel Jukes, John Lee Studios, Marion Price, Helen Trent
Home Economists: Jill Eggleton, Nicola Fowler, Cara Hobday
Step-by-Step Photography Section 2: Karl Adamson
Step-by-Step Home Economist Section 2: Joanna Craig

Photographs on pages 12, 24, 36, 44, 52, 64, 76, 98, 110, 120, 130, 142, 154, 164, 182, 196 and 206 reproduced by permission of ZEFA Picture Library (UK) Ltd.

Material contained in this book has previously appeared in *Classic Indian Cooking, Quick & Easy Indian Cooking, Indian Vegetarian Cooking* and *Indian Side Dishes*.

Note:
Cup measurements in this book are for American cups. Tablespoons are assumed to be 15 ml. Unless otherwise stated, milk is assumed to be full-fat, eggs are standard size 3 and pepper is freshly ground black pepper.

Contents

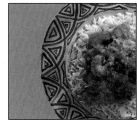

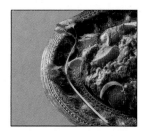
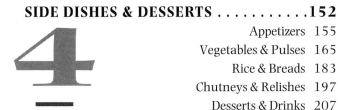

COMPLETE

Indian

COOKING

The cuisine of India offers a whole range of
mouthwatering recipes to the adventurous
cook. Every region of this vast nation has its
own favourite ingredients, flavourings and
methods of cooking, and the variety of dishes
is extensive. There are fiery curries and mild
curries, creamy sauces or dry ones, meat
dishes or vegetarian ones – all using different
blends of aromatic herbs and spices to bring
out the full flavour of the ingredients.

In this book you'll find a complete collection
of recipes for all tastes and occasions.
Whether you want a quick and easy meal or
a complete Indian-style dinner, this book
contains everything you need, right down to
the appetizers and drinks, to capture the
flavour of India.

MILD DISHES

•

MEDIUM DISHES

•

FIERY DISHES

•

FISH DISHES

•

VEGETABLE DISHES

1

CLASSIC
DISHES

CHAPTER ONE

Mild Dishes

❀

Milder dishes are a speciality of northern India, where richer flavours are enjoyed and dairy products are more prevalent. These recipes have a delicate balance of flavours and spice mixes, and extra chilli should not be added to heat them up.

The sauces in this chapter are the kind that the delicate palates of the maharajahs and nazirs of a long ago India might have had prepared for their delectation. Indian cooking can be divided into two definite sections – dishes that are eaten by the ordinary people, prepared by simple methods from basic ingredients, and dishes that are eaten by the upper ranks of society, which are full of subtle spice mixes and sophisticated methods. Kitchens of the wealthy employ a brigade of skilled chefs, one of whom, the *masalchi*, spice grinder, is responsible for the spices. He gathers together all the spices that the chefs will need for the day and grinds them by hand using a pestle and mortar, either individually or mixed together in varying proportions for different mixes and dishes. When all the mixes are right and all the required seeds ground, the spice grinder passes them on to the chefs, who will use skill to get the full flavour out of each spice, adding each one to the dish at the right moment, to achieve a good balance and harmony in the dish.

Opposite: *The Taj Mahal – the essence of India.*

STEP 1

STEP 2

STEP 3

STEP 4

SAFFRON CHICKEN

This is a beautifully aromatic dish, the full fragrance of which brings to mind the opulent days of the maharajahs, with their desert fortresses, lake-side palaces and water gardens.

SERVES 4

large pinch of saffron strands, about 30
  strands
50 ml/2 fl oz/4 tbsp boiling water
4 chicken supremes
3 tbsp ghee
¹/₂ tsp coriander seeds, ground
1 dried bay leaf
2.5 cm/1 inch piece cinnamon stick
30 g/1 oz/1¹/₂ tbsp sultanas (golden raisins)
300 ml/¹/₂ pint/1¹/₄ cups natural yogurt
15 g/¹/₂ oz/2 tbsp flaked (slivered) almonds,
  toasted
salt and pepper

1 Combine the saffron with the boiling water, and leave to steep for 10 minutes.

2 Season the chicken pieces well.

3 Heat the ghee in a large frying pan (skillet), add the chicken pieces and brown on both sides. Cook in batches if necessary. Remove the chicken from the pan.

4 Reduce the heat to medium and add the coriander to the pan, stir once and add the bay leaf, cinnamon stick, sultanas (golden raisins) and the saffron with the soaking water all at once.

5 Return the chicken to the pan. Cover and simmer gently for 40–50 minutes or until the chicken juices run clear when the thickest part of each piece is pierced with a sharp knife. Remove the pan from the heat and gently stir the yogurt into the sauce.

6 Discard the bay leaf and cinnamon stick. Scatter over the toasted almonds and serve.

CHICKEN

The chicken supreme is the breast on the bone; it does not dry out as much as the breast fillet during long cooking, and, in my opinion, has more flavour. Chicken supremes are available from butchers and most supermarkets.

STEP 1

STEP 3

STEP 4

STEP 5

SHAHI MURG

Shahi Murg is a traditional curry cooked in yogurt by a method that is used to make a lot of the sauces in India. They are thickened by long cooking, which separates the yogurt and evaporates the water content. The resulting dishes are delicious, but do take perseverance to make!

SERVES 4

1 tsp cumin seeds
1 tsp coriander seeds
2 tbsp ghee
1 onion, sliced finely
8 small–medium chicken pieces
¹/₂ tsp salt
350 ml/12 fl oz/1¹/₂ cups natural yogurt
120 ml/4 fl oz/¹/₂ cup double cream
1 tbsp ground almonds
¹/₂ tsp garam masala
3 cloves
seeds from 3 green cardamom pods
1 dried bay leaf
60 g/2 oz/¹/₃ cup sultanas (golden raisins)
sprigs of fresh coriander (cilantro) to
   garnish

1 Grind together the cumin and coriander seeds in a spice grinder or a pestle and mortar.

2 Heat half the ghee in a large saucepan and cook the onion over a medium heat for 15 minutes, stirring occasionally, until the onion is very soft.

3 Meanwhile, heat the remaining ghee in a large frying pan (skillet) and brown the chicken pieces well. Add to the onions.

4 Add the ground cumin, ground coriander, salt, yogurt, cream, almonds and garam masala.

5 Bring to a gentle simmer, and add the cloves, cardamom, bay leaf and sultanas (golden raisins).

6 Simmer for 40 minutes until the chicken juices run clear when the thickest part of each piece is pierced with a sharp knife, and the sauce has reduced and thickened.

7 Serve garnished with coriander (cilantro) sprigs.

HANDY HINT

The cloves and bay leaf are not meant to be eaten. I find that it is easier to put them to one side of the plate than to discard them before serving; I never have time to fish about for hours looking for three cloves in a pot of curry, while hungry mouths are waiting!

RASHMI KEBABS

This is a variation on Sheek Kebab (see page 32). A little attention is needed when making the egg 'nets', but the extra effort is worth it, as the effect is very impressive.

STEP 1

STEP 2

STEP 3

STEP 6

SERVES 4

1 red (bell) pepper, chopped coarsely
1 tsp chilli powder
2 tsp coriander seeds
2 tsp cumin seeds
1/2 tsp salt
2 cloves garlic
1/2 tsp ground black pepper
500 g/1 lb/2 cups minced (ground) lamb
4 eggs
oil for deep frying

1 Work the red (bell) pepper, chilli powder, coriander seeds, cumin seeds, salt, garlic and black pepper in a food processor to form a paste. Alternatively, grind the coriander and cumin in a pestle and mortar, chop the red (bell) pepper and garlic very finely and mix with the ground spices, salt, chilli powder and black pepper.

2 Transfer the spice mixture to a bowl and add the lamb and 1 of the eggs. Mix well to evenly distribute the egg and bind the mixture together.

3 Divide the lamb mixture into 8. Shape 1 piece into a ball. Put the ball on a clean plate and gently squash the top with the palm of your hand, to form a patty. Repeat with the remaining pieces. If possible, refrigerate the kebabs for at least 30 minutes.

4 Cook the kebabs under a preheated hot grill (broiler) for 15 minutes, turning once.

5 Meanwhile, make the egg nets. Beat together the remaining eggs. Fill a large frying pan (skillet) with oil to a depth of 5–7.5 cm/2–3 inches. Heat until a cube of bread that is dropped in sizzles in 1 minute.

6 Trickle the egg off the end of a spoon into the oil, criss-crossing the lines in a grid shape. It will take only seconds to cook. Remove and drain on plenty of paper towels. Repeat until all the egg is used. Wrap each kebab in 1–2 egg nets. Serve warm.

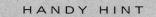

HANDY HINT

Refrigerating the kebabs for at least 30 minutes sets them and ensures that they keep their shape when cooked.

CHICKEN JALFREZI

This is a quick and tasty way to use leftover roast chicken. The sauce can also be used for any cooked poultry, lamb or beef. For extra crunch, add whatever vegetables you have to hand.

STEP 1

SERVES 4

1 tsp mustard oil
3 tbsp vegetable oil
1 large onion, chopped finely
3 garlic cloves, crushed
1 tbsp tomato purée (paste)
2 tomatoes, peeled and chopped
1 tsp ground turmeric
$^{1}/_{2}$ tsp cumin seeds, ground
$^{1}/_{2}$ tsp coriander seeds, ground
$^{1}/_{2}$ tsp chilli powder
$^{1}/_{2}$ tsp garam masala
1 tsp red wine vinegar
1 small red (bell) pepper, chopped
125 g/4 oz/1 cup frozen broad (fava) beans
500 g/1 lb cooked chicken, cut into bite-sized pieces
$^{1}/_{2}$ tsp salt
sprigs of fresh coriander (cilantro) to garnish

STEP 2

ground cumin, ground coriander, chilli powder, garam masala and vinegar to the frying pan (skillet). Stir the mixture until fragrant.

3 Add the red (bell) pepper and broad (fava) beans and stir for 2 minutes until the pepper is softened.

4 Stir in the chicken, and salt to taste. Simmer gently for 6–8 minutes until the chicken is heated through and the beans are tender.

5 Serve garnished with coriander (cilantro) sprigs.

STEP 2

1 Heat the mustard oil in a large, frying pan (skillet) set over a high heat for about 1 minute until it begins to smoke. Add the vegetable oil, reduce the heat and then add the onion and the garlic. Fry oil, garlic and onion until they are golden.

2 Add the tomato purée (paste), chopped tomatoes, turmeric,

USING LEFTOVERS

This dish is an ideal way of making use of leftover poultry – turkey, duck or quail. Any variety of bean works well, but vegetables are just as useful, especially root vegetables, courgettes, potatoes or broccoli. Leafy vegetables will not be so successful.

STEP 3

STEP 1

STEP 2

STEP 3

STEP 5

LAMB BIRYANI

In India this elaborate, beautifully coloured dish is usually served at parties and on festive occasions. This version can be made on any day, festive or not.

SERVES 4

250 g/ 8 oz/ generous 1 cup basmati rice,
   washed and drained
$^1\!/_2$ tsp salt
2 garlic cloves, peeled and left whole
2.5 cm/ 1 inch piece ginger root, grated
4 cloves
$^1\!/_2$ tsp black peppercorns
2 green cardamom pods
1 tsp cumin seeds
1 tsp coriander seeds
2.5 cm/ 1 inch piece cinnamon stick
1 tsp saffron strands
50 ml/ 2 fl oz/ 4 tbsp tepid water
2 tbsp ghee
2 shallots, sliced
$^1\!/_4$ tsp grated nutmeg
$^1\!/_4$ tsp chilli powder
500 g/ 1 lb boneless leg of lamb, cut into
   2.5 cm/ 1 inch cubes
180 ml/ 6 fl oz/ $^3\!/_4$ cup natural yogurt
30 g/ 1 oz/ 2 tbsp sultanas (golden raisins)
30 g / 1 oz/ $^1\!/_4$ cup flaked (slivered) almonds,
   toasted

1 Bring a large saucepan of salted water to the boil. Add the rice and boil for 6 minutes. Drain and set aside.

2 Grind together the garlic, ginger, cloves, peppercorns, cardamom pods, cumin, coriander and cinnamon. Combine saffron and water, and set aside.

3 Heat the ghee in a large saucepan and add shallots. Fry until golden brown then add the ground spice mix, nutmeg and chilli powder. Stir for 1 minute and add the lamb. Cook until evenly browned.

4 Add the yogurt, stirring constantly, then the sultanas (golden raisins) and bring to a simmer. Cook for 40 minutes, stirring occasionally.

5 Carefully pile the rice on the sauce, in a pyramid shape. Trickle the saffron and soaking water over the rice in lines. Cover the pan with a clean tea towel or dish towel and put the lid on. Reduce the heat to low and cook for 10 minutes. Remove the lid and tea towel, and quickly make 3 holes in the rice with a wooden spoon handle, to the level of the sauce, but not touching it. Replace the tea towel and the lid and leave to stand for 5 minutes.

6 Remove the lid and tea towel, lightly fork the rice and serve, sprinkled with the toasted almonds.

CHAPTER TWO

Medium Dishes

❀

The dishes in this chapter are ideal for serving with a selection of pickles and breads at dinner.

There are as many variations on each dish as there are cooks, because each cook has his or her favourite spice mix and method of cooking to produce a flavour that is unique. So you can imagine the variation in Indian cookbooks, each one proudly claiming that its recipes are the best, just as every Indian restaurant proclaims its recipe to be the most original. Although some purists may protest, 'but this is not the *real* cuisine of India', it is what we in the West have come to see as Indian, and unless we are lucky enough to take the few thousand-mile round trip to India, we are unlikely to experience anything different. Therefore, I have included some dishes that you will recognize and may even be familiar with from Indian restaurant menus. These are my recipes, so they may not taste precisely the same as your local curry house, but the key elements are the same. Unlike mild dishes, the heat in these recipes can be varied by increasing or reducing the chilli content.

Opposite: *Mount Annapurna provides a magnificent backdrop for a traditional house in Nepal.*

LAMB DO PYAZA

Do Pyaza usually indicates a dish of meat cooked with plenty of onions. In this recipe the onions are cooked in two different ways: half are fried at the beginning, and the other half are added later to give a more pungent, fresher onion flavour.

STEP 1

SERVES 4

2 tbsp ghee
2 large onions, sliced finely
4 garlic cloves, 2 of them crushed
750 g/1¹/₂ lb boneless lamb shoulder, cut
    into 2.5 cm/1 inch cubes
1 tsp chilli powder
2.5 cm/1 inch piece ginger root, grated
2 fresh green chillies, chopped
¹/₂ tsp ground turmeric
¹/₂ tsp salt and ground black pepper
180 ml/6 fl oz/³/₄ cup natural yogurt
2 cloves
2.5 cm/1 inch piece cinnamon stick
300 ml/¹/₂ pint/1¹/₄ cups water
2 tbsp chopped fresh coriander (cilantro)
3 tbsp lemon juice
naan bread to serve

1 Heat the ghee in a large saucepan and add 1 of the onions and the garlic. Cook for 2–3 minutes, stirring constantly.

2 Add the lamb and brown all over. Remove and set aside.

3 Add the chilli powder, ginger, chillies and turmeric and stir for a further 30 seconds.

STEP 3

4 Add plenty of salt and pepper, the yogurt, cloves, cinnamon and water. Return the lamb to the pan. Bring to the boil then simmer for 10 minutes.

5 Transfer to an ovenproof dish and place uncovered in a preheated oven at 180°C/350°F/Gas Mark 4 for 40 minutes. Check the seasoning.

6 Stir in the remaining onion and cook uncovered for a further 40 minutes.

7 Add the fresh coriander (cilantro) and lemon juice. Serve with naan bread.

STEP 4

ADVANCE PREPARATION

This curry definitely improves if made in advance and then reheated before serving. This develops the flavours and makes them deeper. The dish will also freeze successfully for up to 6 weeks.

STEP 4

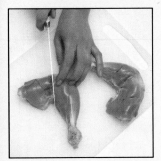

STEP 1

STEP 2

STEP 3

STEP 4

TANDOORI CHICKEN

The traditional Indian tandoor oven is a huge urn. Charcoal is burnt slowly at the bottom of the oven until it becomes a mass of white hot coals. It is then ready for cooking food at a very high temperature. To replicate this in a Western kitchen, cook the tandoori chicken at a very high temperature, preferably on a barbecue.

SERVES 4

8 small chicken portions, skinned
3 dried red chillies
1 tsp salt
2 tsp coriander seeds
2 tbsp lime juice
2 garlic cloves, crushed
2.5 cm/ 1 inch piece ginger root, grated
1 clove
2 tsp garam masala
2 tsp chilli powder
$^{1}/_{2}$ onion, chopped and rinsed
300 ml/$^{1}/_{2}$ pint/ 1$^{1}/_{4}$ cups natural yogurt
1 tbsp chopped fresh coriander (cilantro)
lemon slices to garnish
Cucumber Raita (see page 202) to serve

1 Make 2–3 slashes with a sharp knife in the flesh of the chicken pieces.

2 Crush together the chillies, salt, coriander seeds, lime juice, garlic, ginger and clove. Stir in the garam masala and chilli powder. Transfer to a small saucepan and heat gently until aromatic.

3 Add the onion and fry. Then stir in yogurt and remove pan from heat.

4 Arrange the chicken in a non-metallic dish and pour over the yogurt mixture. Cover and put in the refrigerator to marinate for 4 hours or overnight.

5 Arrange the chicken on a grill (broiler) tray and cook under a preheated very hot grill (broiler) or over a barbecue for 20–30 minutes, turning once, until the chicken juices run clear when the thickest parts of the portions are pierced with a sharp knife.

6 Sprinkle the chicken with chopped fresh coriander (cilantro). Serve hot or cold, garnished with the lemon slices and accompanied by cucumber raita.

LAMB PASANDA

This dish is as close as one gets to the classic curry that springs to mind when Indian cooking is mentioned.

STEP 2

SERVES 4

500 g/ 1 lb boneless lamb shoulder
150 ml/¼ pint/⅔ cup red wine
75 ml/ 3 fl oz/⅓ cup oil
3 garlic cloves, crushed
5 cm/ 2 inch piece ginger root, grated
1 tsp coriander seeds, ground
1 tsp cumin seeds, ground
2 tbsp ghee
1 large onion, chopped
1 tsp garam masala
2 fresh green chillies, halved
300 ml/½ pint/ 1¼ cups natural yogurt
2 tbsp ground almonds
20 whole blanched almonds
salt

1 Cut the lamb into strips 2.5 cm/ 1 inch across and 10 cm/4 inches long. Set aside.

2 Combine the red wine, oil, garlic, ginger, coriander and cumin in a large non-metallic bowl. Stir in the lamb and leave to marinate for 1 hour.

3 Heat the ghee in a frying pan (skillet) and fry the onion until brown.

4 Drain the lamb, reserving the contents of the bowl. Pat the lamb dry with paper towels. Add the lamb to the frying pan (skillet) and stir over a high heat until it is evenly sealed and browned.

STEP 3

5 Add the contents of the bowl to the pan, and bring to a gentle boil. Add the garam masala, chillies, yogurt, ground almonds, whole almonds, and salt to taste. Cover and simmer for 12–15 minutes until the lamb is tender.

STEP 4

MUTTON

In India mutton is often used for curries; it has a lovely full flavour and stands up well to the long cooking of most curries. It is well worth searching for. If you would like to use it for this recipe, marinate boneless shoulder, uncovered, in the refrigerator for 4–5 hours or overnight. Simmer for 1 hour, skimming the surface as necessary to remove any fat, before adding the garam masala, chillies, yogurt and almonds.

STEP 5

SHEEK KEBABS

Sheek Kebabs are delicious cooked over a barbecue. Serve in pitta bread for great party food. The cooked meat can also be chopped into a salad.

STEP 1

STEP 2

STEP 3

STEP 4

SERVES 4–8

1 tsp coriander seeds
1 tsp cumin seeds
1 clove
2.5 cm/1 inch piece ginger root, chopped
1 tsp ground turmeric
1 fresh red chilli, deseeded and chopped
$^{1}/_{2}$ tsp ground cinnamon
1 tsp ground black pepper
$^{1}/_{2}$ tsp salt
125 g/4 oz/$^{1}/_{2}$ cup minced (ground) beef
350 g/12 oz/1$^{1}/_{2}$ cups minced (ground) lamb
1 onion, chopped finely
1 egg

TO SERVE:
salad
Cucumber Raita (see page 202)

1 Grind together the coriander, cumin, clove and ginger in a pestle and mortar. Mix in the turmeric, chilli, cinnamon, pepper and salt.

2 Combine the spice mixture with the beef, lamb and onion.

3 Make a well in the centre of the meat mixture, add the egg and mix in thoroughly.

4 Press one-eighth of the meat mixture around an oiled skewer, to form a shape about 10 cm/4 inches long and 2.5 cm/1 inch thick. Repeat with the remaining meat mixture.

5 If possible, leave to rest in the refrigerator for at least 1 hour.

6 Cook the kebabs under a preheated medium grill (broiler) for about 20 minutes, turning once or twice, until the meat juices run clear when the thickest part of the meat is pierced with the point of a sharp knife.

7 Serve with salad and cucumber raita.

WOODEN SKEWERS

Wooden skewers should be soaked in hot water for 20 minutes before they are used, to prevent them from burning.

STEP 2

STEP 4

STEP 6

STEP 7

ROGAN JOSH

Rogan Josh is one of the best-known curries and is a great favourite in restaurants. The title means 'red curry', the red being provided by the chillies.

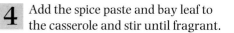

SERVES 6

2 tbsp ghee
1 kg/ 2 lb braising steak, cut into 2.5 cm/
    1 inch cubes
1 onion, chopped finely
3 garlic cloves
2.5 cm/ 1 inch piece ginger root, grated
4 fresh red chillies, chopped
4 green cardamom pods
4 cloves
2 tsp coriander seeds
2 tsp cumin seeds
1 tsp paprika
1 tsp salt
1 dried bay leaf
120 ml / 4 fl oz/ $^{1}/_{2}$ cup natural yogurt
2.5 cm/ 1 inch piece cinnamon stick
150 ml/ $^{1}/_{4}$ pint/ $^{2}/_{3}$ cups hot water
$^{1}/_{4}$ tsp garam masala
pepper

1 Heat the ghee in a large flameproof casserole and brown the meat in batches. Set aside in a bowl.

2 Add the onion to the ghee and stir over a high heat for 3–4 minutes.

3 Grind together the garlic, ginger, chillies, cardamom, cloves, coriander, cumin, paprika and salt.

4 Add the spice paste and bay leaf to the casserole and stir until fragrant.

5 Return the meat and any juices in the bowl to the casserole and simmer for 2–3 minutes.

6 Gradually stir the yogurt into the casserole so that the sauce keeps simmering.

7 Stir in the cinnamon and hot water, and pepper to taste.

8 Cover and cook in a preheated oven at 180°C/ 350°F/ Gas Mark 4 for 1¼ hours, stirring frequently, until the meat is very tender and the sauce is slightly reduced.

9 Discard the cinnamon stick and stir in the garam masala. Remove surplus oil from the surface of the casserole before serving.

CHAPTER THREE

Fiery Dishes

❀

These recipes are for more experienced curry eaters. The spice mixes in these dishes take as much balancing and harmonizing as in the mild dishes where the only flavours are the spices. In these hotter dishes, the spices have to provide a deeper flavour, such as the sweetness in Lamb Bhuna or the sharpness in Vindaloo Curry.

If you are serving a selection of dishes for an Indian-style dinner, include a fiery curry for those who feel that the other dishes are too mild and to provide the more timid guests with a wider experience. Be sure to offer plenty of rice, bread, raitas and vegetable dishes to accompany a hot curry. These are more effective at diluting the heat than water, and allow the fuller flavours to be appreciated. In fact, drinking water is the wrong thing to do. However, in my experience, if somebody selects a fiery curry by mistake, while their tongue is on fire and their eyes are on stalks, the last thing they want to hear is 'Just eat some rice, and you will be fine'; they would rather be passed the water jug – no glass, just the whole jug!

The flavours and heat in a fiery dish smooth out if it is made in advance then reheated when required.

Opposite: The teeming riverside at Benares (also known as Varanasi) on the River Ganges.

STEP 1

STEP 3

STEP 4

STEP 5

LAMB BHUNA

The pungent flavours of the chillies in this curry should not hide the flavours of the other spices. However, you do have to become accustomed to the strong chillies before these subtle flavours can be appreciated!

SERVES 4–6

1 onion, chopped
2 garlic cloves
3 tomatoes, peeled and chopped
1 tsp malt vinegar
1 tbsp oil
750 g/1¹/₂ lb lean boneless lamb, cut into
    4 cm/1¹/₂ inch cubes
2 tsp coriander seeds, ground
1 tsp cumin seeds, ground
2 dried red chillies, chopped
3 fresh green chillies, chopped
¹/₂ tsp ground turmeric
30 g/1 oz/2 tbsp creamed coconut
50 ml/2 fl oz/4 tbsp water
1 tsp garam masala
salt and pepper
fresh coriander (cilantro) leaves to garnish

1 Purée the onion, garlic, tomatoes and vinegar in a food processor or blender. Alternatively, chop the vegetables finely by hand, then mix with the vinegar. Set aside.

2 Heat the oil in a large frying pan (skillet) and brown the meat for 5–10 minutes. Remove and set aside.

3 Reduce the heat beneath the pan and add the ground coriander seeds, cumin, chillies and turmeric. Stir continuously until the spices are fragrant.

4 Increase the heat again and add the onion mixture. Stir-fry for 5 minutes until nearly dry.

5 Return the meat to the pan. Combine the coconut and water and add to the pan. Simmer for 45–60 minutes until the meat is tender. Stir in the garam masala and season to taste.

6 Serve garnished with fresh coriander (cilantro) leaves.

CREAMED COCONUT

Creamed coconut can be bought in block form and is extremely convenient to keep on hand. Coconut milk can be made by dissolving creamed coconut in an equal quantity of tepid water. The addition of creamed coconut or coconut milk adds richness to a dish and, if used in small quantities, gives a good depth of flavour.

CHICKEN TIKKA MASALA

Serve this very rich dish with an array of accompaniments to provide a balance and to neutralize the fiery flavours. Try serving the chicken with mango chutney, Lime Pickle (see page 200) and Cucumber Raita (see page 202). Add poppadoms and rice to make a delicious meal.

STEP 1

SERVES 4

½ onion, chopped coarsely
60 g/2 oz/3 tbsp tomato purée (paste)
1 tsp cumin seeds
2.5 cm/1 inch piece ginger root, chopped
3 tbsp lemon juice
2 garlic cloves, crushed
2 tsp chilli powder
750 g/1½ lb boneless chicken
salt and pepper
sprigs of fresh mint to garnish

MASALA SAUCE:
2 tbsp ghee
1 onion, sliced
1 tbsp black onion seeds
3 garlic cloves, crushed
2 fresh green chillies, chopped
200 g/7 oz can tomatoes
120 ml/4 fl oz/½ cup natural yogurt
120 ml/4 fl oz/½ cup coconut milk
1 tbsp chopped fresh coriander (cilantro)
1 tbsp chopped fresh mint
2 tbsp lemon or lime juice
½ tsp garam masala

1 Combine the onion, tomato purée (paste), cumin, ginger, lemon juice, garlic, chilli powder and salt and pepper in a food processor or blender and then transfer to a bowl. Alternatively, grind the cumin in a pestle and mortar and transfer to a bowl. Finely chop the onion and ginger and stir into the bowl with the tomato purée (paste), lemon juice, salt and pepper, garlic and chilli powder.

2 Cut chicken into 4 cm/1½ inch cubes. Stir into the bowl and leave to marinate for 2 hours.

3 Make the masala sauce. Heat the ghee in a large saucepan, add the onion and stir over a medium heat for 5 minutes. Add the onion seeds, garlic and chillies and cook until fragrant.

4 Add the tomatoes, yogurt and coconut milk, bring to the boil, then simmer for 20 minutes.

5 Meanwhile, divide the chicken evenly between 8 oiled skewers and cook under a preheated very hot grill (broiler) for 15 minutes, turning frequently. Remove the chicken from the skewers and add to the sauce. Stir in the fresh coriander (cilantro), mint, lemon or lime juice, and garam masala. Serve garnished with mint sprigs.

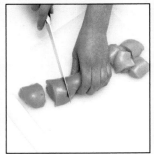

STEP 2

STEP 3

STEP 4

VINDALOO CURRY

Vindaloo is the classic fiery curry that originates in Goa. The 'vin' in the title refers to the vinegar that is added to tenderize the meat. The vinegar has to be balanced with other flavours, such as chilli, and does not work so well with any meat other than pork.

STEP 2

STEP 3

STEP 4

STEP 5

SERVES 4–6

100 ml/3¹/₂ fl oz/scant ¹/₂ cup oil
1 large onion, sliced into half rings
120 ml/4 fl oz/¹/₂ cup white wine vinegar
300 ml/¹/₂ pint/1¹/₄ cups water
750 g/1¹/₂ lb boneless pork shoulder, diced
2 tsp cumin seeds
4 dried red chillies
1 tsp black peppercorns
6 green cardamom pods
2.5 cm/1 inch piece cinnamon stick
1 tsp black mustard seeds
3 cloves
1 tsp fenugreek seeds
2 tbsp ghee
4 garlic cloves, chopped finely
3.5 cm/1¹/₂ inch piece ginger root, chopped finely
1 tbsp coriander seeds, ground
2 tomatoes, peeled and chopped
250 g/8 oz potato, cut into 1 cm/¹/₂ inch cubes
1 tsp light brown sugar
¹/₂ tsp ground turmeric
salt

TO SERVE:
basmati rice
pickles

1 Heat the oil in a large saucepan and fry the onion until golden brown. Set aside.

2 Combine 2 tablespoons of the vinegar with 1 tablespoon of the water in a large bowl, add the pork and stir together well. Set aside.

3 In a food processor work the onions, cumin, chillies, peppercorns, cardamom, cinnamon, mustard seeds, cloves and fenugreek to a paste. Alternatively, grind the ingredients together in a pestle and mortar. Transfer to a bowl and add the remaining vinegar.

4 Heat the ghee in a frying pan (skillet) or casserole and cook the pork until it is browned on all sides.

5 Stir in the garlic, ginger and ground coriander until fragrant, then add the tomatoes, potato, brown sugar, turmeric and remaining water. Add salt to taste and bring to the boil. Stir in the spice paste, cover and reduce the heat, and simmer for 1 hour until the pork is tender.

6 Serve with basmati rice and pickles.

CHAPTER FOUR

Fish Dishes

❦

There is a vast array of fresh seafood in southern India, Bengal, Calcutta and its environs, and as far north as Darjeeling. North of Calcutta rivers and streams flow from the Himalayas. The water is very clean and pure and a great variety of river fish is caught. Lake fish are also enjoyed when available.

The same varieties of fish cannot be readily obtained in the West, but I have adapted the recipes for fish that can be bought more easily. However, if you are ever near an Indian supermarket, it is worth a look in just to see the amazing variety of warm water fish that is frozen and exported from India, such as huge catfish, pomfret, eels and enormous uncooked prawns (shrimp). Lake and river fish are also exported, and such well-known fish as carp, perch, pike and baby eels (elvers) are readily available.

Although fresh uncooked tiger prawns (shrimp) are usually expensive, frozen packs of them can be found in most supermarkets and freezer stores, and it is these that I have used in the prawn (shrimp) recipes because they have more flavour and are more versatile than ready-cooked prawns (shrimp).

Opposite: *Palms sway in the breeze on Anjuna beach in Goa.*

STEP 1

STEP 2

STEP 3

STEP 4

PRAWN (SHRIMP) DANSAK

Parsis are, in the context of India's history, relatively new, having arrived only 500 years ago. The Parsi cuisine favours elaborate preparations, usually done by the household cooks. The lentil purée sauce in this recipe is of Parsi origin and popular throughout India.

SERVES 4–6

750 g/1½ lb uncooked tiger prawns
   (shrimp) in their shells or 650 g/1 lb 5 oz
   peeled tiger prawns (shrimp), or cooked,
   peeled Atlantic prawns (shrimp)
1 tsp salt
1 dried bay leaf
3 garlic cloves
90 g/3 oz/⅓ cup split yellow peas, soaked
   for 1 hour in cold water and drained
60 g/2 oz/¼ cup red lentils
1 carrot, chopped
1 potato, cut into large dice
3 tbsp drained canned sweetcorn
3 tbsp oil
2 onions, chopped
½ tsp yellow mustard seeds
1½ tsp coriander seeds, ground
½ tsp cumin seeds, ground
½ tsp fenugreek seeds, ground
1½ tsp ground turmeric
1 dried red chilli
425 g/14 oz can tomatoes
½ tsp garam masala
3 tbsp chopped fresh coriander (cilantro)
2 tbsp chopped fresh mint

1 Reserve a few of the prawns (shrimp) for garnish and peel the rest. Set aside. Cook those for the garnish in boiling water for 3–5 minutes.

2 Fill a large saucepan with water and add the salt, bay leaf, 1 garlic clove and the split yellow peas. Bring to the boil and cook for 15 minutes. Add the red lentils, carrot and potato and cook, uncovered, for a further 15 minutes. Drain, discarding the garlic and bay leaf.

3 Purée the cooked vegetables with the sweetcorn in a blender or food processor. Alternatively, use a potato masher to break down the lumps.

4 Crush the remaining garlic. Heat the oil in a large saucepan and cook the onion and garlic for 3–4 minutes. Add the mustard seeds and when they start to pop, stir in the ground coriander, cumin, fenugreek, turmeric and chilli. Add the peeled prawns (shrimp) and stir over a high heat for 1–2 minutes.

5 Add the tomatoes and the puréed vegetables, and gently simmer, uncovered, for 30–40 minutes. Stir in the garam masala and taste for seasoning.

6 Serve, sprinkled with the fresh coriander (cilantro) and mint, and garnished with reserved prawns (shrimp).

STEP 1

STEP 1

STEP 2

STEP 4

MASALA FRIED FISH

Frying fish is classically Indian, although it does not always spring to mind when thinking of Indian food.

SERVES 4–8

8 plaice or other white fish fillets, about
    125–150 g/4–5 oz each
1 tbsp ground turmeric
2 tbsp plain (all-purpose) flour
salt
1/2 tsp black peppercorns, ground
1 tsp chilli powder
1 tbsp coriander seeds, ground
1 garlic clove, crushed
2 tsp garam masala
oil for deep frying

TO GARNISH:
chilli powder
lemon wedges

1 To skin the fish fillets, lay the fillet skin side down with the tail nearest you. Hold the tail end between your thumb and forefinger. Hold a sharp knife at a shallow angle to the fish. Holding the fish firmly, make an angled cut between the flesh and the skin, then continue to cut the flesh away from the skin until the flesh is free.

2 In a shallow dish, combine the turmeric, flour, salt, peppercorns, chilli powder, coriander seeds, garlic and garam masala. Mix well.

3 Fill a shallow saucepan or a deep frying pan (skillet) with oil to a depth of 5–7 cm/2–3 inches, and heat to 180°C/350°F or until a cube of bread browns in 30 seconds.

4 Turn the fish fillets in the spice mix until well coated.

5 Deep fry the fish fillets for about 3–5 minutes, turning often until the fish flakes with a fork. Drain on plenty of paper towels.

6 Serve sprinkled with chilli powder, garnished with lemon wedges, and accompanied by a selection of pickles and chutneys.

DEEP FRYING

When deep frying, it is important to use oil at the correct temperature. If the oil is too hot, the outside of the food will burn, as will the spices, before the inside is cooked. If the oil is too cool, the food will be sodden with oil before a crisp crust forms. Draining on paper towels is essential, as they absorb excess oil and moisture.

PRAWN (SHRIMP) BHUNA

This is a fiery recipe with subtle undertones. As the flavour of the prawns should be noticeable, the spices should not take over this dish. The term 'Bhuna' refers to the method of bringing out the full flavours of the spices by heating them in a pan before adding the other ingredients.

STEP 1

STEP 2

STEP 3

STEP 4

SERVES 4–6

2 dried red chillies, deseeded if liked
3 fresh green chillies, finely chopped
1 tsp ground turmeric
2 tsp white wine vinegar
1/2 tsp salt
3 garlic cloves, crushed
1/2 tsp ground black pepper
1 tsp paprika
500 g/1 lb uncooked peeled king prawns
    (shrimp)
4 tbsp oil
1 onion, chopped very finely
180 ml/6 fl oz/3/4 cup water
2 tbsp lemon juice
2 tsp garam masala
sprigs of fresh coriander (cilantro) to
    garnish

1 Combine the chillies, turmeric, vinegar, salt, garlic, pepper and paprika in a non-metallic bowl. Stir in the prawns and set aside for 10 minutes.

2 Heat the oil in a large frying pan (skillet) or wok, add the onion and fry for 3–4 minutes until the onion is soft.

3 Add the prawns (shrimp) and the contents of the bowl to the pan and stir-fry over a high heat for 2 minutes.

4 Reduce the heat, add the water and boil for 10 minutes, stirring occasionally, until the water is evaporated and the curry is fragrant.

5 Stir in the lemon juice and garam masala.

6 Serve garnished with fresh coriander (cilantro) sprigs.

FLAVOUR FROM HERBS AND SPICES

To get the full flavour from any spices they must be heated first. This also applies to dried herbs. To make raita with dried herbs, take 3 tsp of dried mint and put it into a dry pan, warm it through very gently until you can start to smell the mint. Remove it from the heat and add 120 ml/4 fl oz/1/2 cup natural yogurt and salt to taste. Transfer to a serving dish.

CHAPTER FIVE

Vegetable Dishes

❀

By applying myriad methods born of a centuries-old tradition of vegetarianism, Indian cooks turn the simplest vegetables into the most extraordinary feasts. Many of these cooking methods are completely alien to us, but they result in dishes which are both a joy to eat and nourishing to mind and body.

Indian vegetarianism is due mainly to the predominant Hindu religion, with its reverence for animals – especially cows – and its ideal of harmonizing the diet with the needs of the soul. A vegetarian diet is also followed because vegetable cropping is a more efficient use of land than keeping animals for food.

Although we may be used to eating vegetables with Indian meals in restaurants, restaurant cuisine here differs markedly from native cuisine. In India vegetables are relied on to play a leading role in a meal, for example, in a *bhaji* (a dry curry), or puréed in a *bhartha*.

Vegetable curries are flavoured simply and the spices and sauces can be transferred easily between vegetables. For example, the flavourings in one dal stew can easily be used with other available pulses and you can experiment with your own spice mixes when you have some vegetables to cook.

Opposite: Farmers threshing rice with oxen at a farm in Nepal.

STEP 1

STEP 2

STEP 3

STEP 4

CHANNA DAL

This is a dish to consider next time you wish to prepare a dal. Many types of dal – dried pulses and lentils – are used in India, but fewer are available elsewhere. Dals can be cooked in similar ways, but the soaking and cooking times do vary, so check the pack for instructions.

SERVES 4–6

2 tbsp ghee
1 large onion, chopped finely
1 garlic clove, crushed
1 tbsp grated ginger root
1 tbsp cumin seeds, ground
2 tsp coriander seeds, ground
1 dried red chilli
2.5 cm/1 inch piece cinnamon stick
1 tsp salt
$\frac{1}{2}$ tsp ground turmeric
250 g/8 oz/1 cup split yellow peas, soaked
   in cold water for 1 hour and drained
425 g/14 oz can tomatoes
300 ml/$\frac{1}{2}$ pint/1$\frac{1}{4}$ cups water
2 tsp garam masala

1 Heat the ghee in a large saucepan, add the onion, garlic and ginger and fry for 3–4 minutes until the onion has softened slightly.

2 Add the cumin, coriander, chilli, cinnamon, salt and turmeric, then stir in the split peas until well mixed.

3 Add the contents of the can of tomatoes, breaking the tomatoes up slightly with the back of the spoon.

4 Add the water and bring to the boil. Reduce the heat to very low and simmer, uncovered, for about 40 minutes, stirring occasionally, until most of the liquid has been absorbed and the split peas are tender. Skim the surface occasionally with a perforated spoon to remove any scum.

5 Gradually stir in the garam masala, tasting after each addition, until it is of the required flavour.

HANDY HINTS

Use a non-stick saucepan if you have one, because the mixture is quite dense and does stick to the bottom of the pan occasionally. If the dal is overstirred the split peas will break up and the dish will not have much texture or bite.

ALOO CHAT

Aloo Chat (chat means salad) is one of a variety of Indian foods served at any time of the day. Indians are expert at combining flavours and textures in subtle mixes designed to satisfy and stimulate the appetite.

STEP 1

SERVES 4

125 g/4 oz/generous ¹/₂ cup chick-peas (garbanzo beans), soaked overnight in cold water and drained
1 dried red chilli
500 g/1 lb waxy potatoes, such as red-skinned or Cyprus potatoes, boiled in their skins and peeled
1 tsp cumin seeds
1 tsp black peppercorns
2 tsp salt
¹/₂ tsp dried mint
¹/₂ tsp chilli powder
¹/₂ tsp ground ginger
2 tsp mango powder
120 ml/4 fl oz/¹/₂ cup natural yogurt
oil for deep frying
4 poppadoms
Cucumber Raita (see page 202) to serve

1 Boil the chick-peas (garbanzo beans) with the chilli in plenty of water for about 1 hour until tender. Drain.

2 Cut the potatoes into 2.5 cm/ 1 inch dice and mix into the chick-peas (garbanzo beans) while they are still warm. Set aside.

3 Grind together the cumin, peppercorns and salt in a spice grinder or pestle and mortar. Stir in the mint, chilli powder, ginger and mango powder.

4 Put a small saucepan or frying pan (skillet) over a low heat and add the spice mix. Stir until fragrant and immediately remove from the heat.

5 Stir half of the spice mix into the chick-peas (garbanzo beans) and potatoes, and stir the yogurt into the other half.

6 Cook the poppadoms according to the pack instructions. Drain on plenty of paper towels. Break into bite-size pieces and stir into the potatoes and chick-peas (garbanzo beans), spoon over the spiced yogurt and serve with the cucumber raita.

STEP 2

STEP 3

VARIATION

Instead of chick-peas (garbanzo beans), diced tropical fruits can be stirred into the potato and spice mix; add a little lemon juice to balance the sweetness.

STEP 4

STEP 2

STEP 2

STEP 3

STEP 3

BOMBAY POTATOES

Although virtually unknown in India, this dish is a very popular item on Indian restaurant menus in other parts of the world. It works best when served with rice as a vegetable dish, rather than instead of rice. The success of the recipe rests on using waxy potatoes such as red-skinned or Cyprus potatoes, because they do not break up readily.

SERVES 4

1 kg/2 lb waxy potatoes, peeled
2 tbsp ghee
1 tsp Panch Poran spice mix (see below)
3 tsp ground turmeric
2 tbsp tomato purée (paste)
300 ml/¹/₂ pint/1¹/₄ cups natural yogurt
salt
chopped fresh coriander (cilantro) to garnish

1 Put the whole potatoes into a large saucepan of salted cold water, bring to the boil, then simmer until the potatoes are just cooked but not to soft; the time depends on the size of the potato, but an average-sized one should take about 15 minutes.

2 Put the ghee into a saucepan over a medium heat, and add the panch poran, turmeric, tomato purée (paste), yogurt and salt. Bring to the boil, and simmer, uncovered, for 5 minutes.

3 Drain the potatoes and cut each into 4 pieces.

4 Add the potatoes to the pan and cook with a lid on. Transfer to an ovenproof casserole, cover and cook in a preheated oven at 180°C/350°F/Gas Mark 4 for about 40 minutes, until the potatoes are tender and the sauce has thickened a little.

5 Sprinkle liberally with fresh chopped coriander (cilantro) and serve immediately.

PANCH PORAN SPICE MIX

Panch poran spice mix can be bought from Asian or Indian grocery stores, or make your own from equal quantities of cumin seeds, fennel seeds, mustard seeds, nigella seeds and fenugreek seeds.

BOILING VEGETABLES

Cooking vegetables and rice in water at a rolling boil does not speed the cooking, and when cooking potatoes it just makes them break up and quickly go to a mush. Unless a recipe specifies a rolling boil, I recommend keeping the water at a simmer once it has come up to the boil.

TARKA DAL

*This is just one version of many dals that are served throughout India;
in the absence of regular supplies of meat, they form a
staple part of the diet.*

STEP 1

STEP 2

STEP 3

STEP 3

SERVES 4

2 tbsp ghee
2 shallots, sliced
1 tsp yellow mustard seeds
2 garlic cloves, crushed
8 fenugreek seeds
1 cm/$^1/_2$ inch piece ginger root, grated
$^1/_2$ tsp salt
125 g/4 oz/$^1/_2$ cup red lentils
1 tbsp tomato purée (paste)
600 ml/1 pint/2$^1/_2$ cups water
2 tomatoes, peeled and chopped
1 tbsp lemon juice
4 tbsp chopped fresh coriander (cilantro)
$^1/_2$ tsp chilli powder
$^1/_2$ tsp garam masala
naan bread to serve (optional)

1 Heat half of the ghee in a large saucepan, and add the shallots. Cook for 2–3 minutes over a high heat, then add the mustard seeds. Cover the pan until the seeds begin to pop.

2 Immediately remove the lid from the pan and add the garlic, fenugreek, ginger and salt.

3 Stir once and add the lentils, tomato purée (paste) and water and simmer gently for 10 minutes.

4 Stir in the tomatoes, lemon juice, and coriander (cilantro) and simmer for a further 4–5 minutes until the lentils are tender.

5 Transfer to a serving dish. Heat the remaining ghee in a small saucepan until it starts to bubble. Remove from the heat and stir in the chilli powder and garam masala. Immediately pour over the tarka dal and serve with naan bread, if liked.

DALS

The flavours in a dal can be altered to suit your personal taste; for example, for added heat, add more chilli powder or chillies, or add fennel seeds for a pleasant aniseed flavour.

To make a dal stew into a single-dish meal, add a combination of vegetables, such as fried aubergine cubes (eggplant), courgettes (zucchini), carrots, or any firm vegetable that you have to hand; pumpkin is particularly successful.

SOUPS & STARTERS

•

MAIN DISHES

•

ACCOMPANIMENTS

CHAPTER SIX

Soups & Starters

❀

If a dessert is the grand finale to a meal then a starter is the overture, and should be orchestrated to tease the tastebuds and tempt the appetite. The repertoire of vegetarian Indian dishes to fulfil this role are fortunately wide and varied. Soups are a natural choice for the prepare-ahead cook and can be made thick and hearty with pulses like beans and lentils to satisfy large appetites. Some soups, like Indian Bean Soup and Spicy Dal and Carrot Soup, will also double up beautifully as light lunch dishes. Others provide a lighter, more refreshing start, as in Minted Pea and Yogurt Soup.

In India, starters are rarely served as such, and would instead accompany a meal. These typical dishes do, however, fill the role of appetizers and are just perfect to serve with drinks at informal buffet parties. Vegetable and Cashew Samosas and Spiced Corn and Nut Mix make superb alternatives to the predictable peanuts and crisps usually offered with drinks.

Opposite: *Transporting supplies by canoe in Kerala.*

INDIAN BEAN SOUP

A thick and hearty soup, nourishing and substantial enough to serve as a main meal with wholemeal bread. Black-eye beans (peas) are used here, but red kidney beans may be added to the mixture if preferred.

STEP 1

STEP 2

STEP 3

STEP 4

SERVES 4–6

4 tbsp ghee or vegetable oil
2 onions, chopped
250 g/8 oz/1¹/₂ cups potato, cut into chunks
250 g/8 oz/1¹/₂ cups parsnip, cut into chunks
250 g/8 oz/1¹/₂ cups turnip or swede, cut into chunks
2 celery sticks, trimmed and sliced
2 courgettes (zucchini), trimmed and sliced
1 green (bell) pepper, cut into 1 cm/¹/₂ inch pieces
2 garlic cloves, crushed
2 tsp ground coriander
1 tbsp paprika
1 tbsp mild curry paste
1.25 litres/2 pints/5 cups vegetable stock
475 g/15 oz can black-eye beans (peas), drained and rinsed
salt
chopped fresh coriander (cilantro) to garnish (optional)

1 Heat the ghee or oil in a saucepan, add all the prepared vegetables, except the courgettes (zucchini) and green (bell) pepper, and cook over a moderate heat for 5 minutes, stirring frequently. Add the garlic, coriander, paprika and curry paste and cook for 1 minute, stirring.

2 Stir in the stock and season with salt to taste. Bring to the boil, cover and simmer gently for 25 minutes, stirring occasionally.

3 Stir in the black-eye beans (peas), sliced courgettes (zucchini) and green (bell) pepper, cover and continue cooking for a further 15 minutes or until all the vegetables are tender.

4 Purée 300 ml/¹/₂ pint/1¹/₄ cups of the soup mixture (about 2 ladlefuls) in a food processor or blender or push through a sieve (strainer). Return the puréed mixture to the soup in the saucepan and reheat until piping hot. Sprinkle with chopped coriander (cilantro), if using, and serve hot.

VARIATION

For a thinner, broth-type consistency to the soup, do not purée the two ladlefuls of mixture as instructed at step 4. The flavour of this soup improves if made the day before it is required, as this allows time for all the flavours to blend and develop.

MINTED PEA & YOGURT SOUP

A deliciously refreshing soup that is full of goodness. It is also extremely tasty served chilled, in which case you may like to thin the consistency a little more with extra stock, yogurt or milk, as wished.

STEP 1

SERVES 6

2 tbsp vegetable ghee or oil
2 onions, chopped coarsely
250 g/8 oz potato, chopped coarsely
2 garlic cloves
2.5 cm/1 inch piece ginger root, chopped
1 tsp ground coriander
1 tsp ground cumin
1 tbsp plain (all-purpose) flour
900 ml/1½ pints/3½ cups vegetable stock
500 g/1 lb frozen peas
2–3 tbsp chopped fresh mint, to taste
150 ml/¼ pint/⅔ cup strained thick yogurt
½ tsp cornflour (cornstarch)
300 ml/½ pint/1¼ cups milk
salt and pepper
a little extra yogurt to serve (optional)
mint sprigs to garnish

1 Heat the ghee or oil in a saucepan, add the onions and potato and cook gently for 3 minutes. Stir in the garlic, ginger, coriander, cumin and flour and cook for 1 minute, stirring.

2 Add the stock, peas and mint and bring to the boil, stirring. Reduce the heat, cover and simmer gently for 15 minutes or until the vegetables are tender.

3 Purée the soup, in batches, in a blender or food processor, or press through a sieve (strainer). Return the mixture to the pan and season with salt and pepper to taste. Blend the yogurt with the cornflour (cornstarch) and stir into the soup.

4 Add the milk and bring almost to the boil, stirring all the time. Cook very gently for 2 minutes. Serve hot, with a swirl of extra yogurt, if wished, and garnished with mint sprigs.

STEP 2

STEP 3

COOK'S TIP

The yogurt is mixed with a little cornflour (cornstarch) before being added to the hot soup – this helps to stabilize the yogurt and prevents it separating when heated.

STEP 4

STEP 1

STEP 2

STEP 3

STEP 4

SPICY DAL & CARROT SOUP

This delicious, warming and nutritious soup uses split red lentils and carrots as the two main ingredients and includes a selection of spices to give it a 'kick'. It is simple to make and extremely good to eat.

SERVES 6

125 g/4 oz split red lentils
1.25 litres/2¼ pints/5 cups vegetable stock
350 g/12 oz carrots, sliced
2 onions, chopped
250 g/8 oz can chopped tomatoes
2 garlic cloves, chopped
2 tbsp vegetable ghee or oil
1 tsp ground cumin
1 tsp ground coriander
1 fresh green chilli, deseeded and chopped, or
    use 1 tsp minced chilli (from a jar)
½ tsp ground turmeric
1 tbsp lemon juice
300 ml/½ pint/1¼ cups milk
2 tbsp chopped fresh coriander
    (cilantro)
salt
yogurt to serve

1 Place the lentils in a sieve (strainer) and wash well under cold running water. Drain and place in a large saucepan with 900 ml/1½ pints/3½ cups of the stock, the carrots, onions, tomatoes and garlic. Bring the mixture to the boil, reduce the heat, cover and simmer for 30 minutes or until the vegetables and lentils are tender.

2 Meanwhile, heat the ghee or oil in a small pan, add the cumin, coriander, chilli and turmeric and fry gently for 1 minute. Remove from the heat and stir in the lemon juice and salt to taste.

3 Purée the soup in batches in a blender or food processor or press through a sieve (strainer). Return the soup to the saucepan, add the spice mixture and the remaining 300 ml/ ½ pint/1¼ cups stock or water and simmer for 10 minutes.

4 Add the milk, taste and adjust the seasoning, if necessary. Stir in the chopped coriander (cilantro) and reheat gently. Serve hot, with a swirl of yogurt.

VARIATION

As this soup has quite a hot and spicy flavour, it may be wise to omit or at least reduce the amount of chilli in the recipe when serving it to children. A spoonful of natural yogurt, swirled into each serving of soup makes it extra nutritious and delicious.

STEP 1

STEP 2

STEP 3

STEP 4

SPICED CORN & NUT MIX

A tasty mixture of buttery-spiced nuts, raisins and popcorn to enjoy as a snack or with pre-dinner drinks.

SERVES 6

2 tbsp vegetable oil
60 g/2 oz/¼ cup popping corn
60 g/2 oz/¼ cup butter
1 garlic clove, crushed
60 g/2 oz/⅓ cup unblanched almonds
60 g/2 oz/½ cup unsalted cashews
60 g/2 oz/½ cup unsalted peanuts
1 tsp Worcestershire sauce
1 tsp curry powder or paste
¼ tsp chilli powder
60 g/2 oz/⅓ cup seedless raisins
salt

1 Heat the oil in a saucepan. Add the popping corn, stir well, then cover and cook over a fairly high heat for 3–5 minutes, holding the saucepan lid firmly and shaking the pan frequently until the popping stops.

2 Turn the popped corn into a dish, discarding any unpopped corn kernels.

3 Melt the butter in a frying pan, add the garlic, almonds, cashews and peanuts, then stir in the Worcestershire sauce, curry powder or paste and chilli powder and cook over medium heat for 2–3 minutes, stirring frequently.

4 Remove the pan from the heat and stir in the raisins and popped corn. Season with salt to taste and mix well. Transfer to a serving bowl and serve warm or cold.

VARIATIONS

Use a mixture of any unsalted nuts of your choice – walnuts, pecans, hazelnuts, Brazils, macadamia nuts and pine kernels (nuts) are all delicious prepared this way. For a less fiery flavour omit the curry powder and chilli powder and add instead 1 tsp cumin seeds, 1 tsp ground coriander and ½ tsp paprika. Sprinkle with 1–2 tbsp of chopped fresh coriander (cilantro) just before serving.

VEGETABLE & CASHEW SAMOSAS

These delicious little fried pastries are really quite simple to make.
Serve them hot as a starter to an Indian meal or cold as
a tasty picnic or lunch-box snack.

STEP 1

MAKES 12

350 g/12 oz potatoes, diced
125 g/4 oz frozen peas
3 tbsp vegetable oil
1 onion, chopped
2.5 cm/1 inch piece ginger root, chopped
1 garlic clove, crushed
1 tsp garam masala
2 tsp mild curry paste
1/2 tsp cumin seeds
2 tsp lemon juice
60 g/2 oz/1/2 cup unsalted cashews, chopped
    coarsely
vegetable oil, for shallow frying
salt
sprigs of fresh coriander (cilantro) to
    garnish

PASTRY:
250 g/8 oz/2 cups plain flour
60 g/2 oz/1/4 cup butter
75 ml/3 fl oz/5 tbsp warm milk

1 Cook the potatoes in a saucepan of boiling, salted water for 5 minutes. Add the peas and cook for a further 4 minutes or until the potato is tender. Drain well. Heat the oil in a frying pan (skillet), add the onion, potato and pea mixture, ginger, garlic and spices and fry for 2 minutes. Stir in the lemon juice and cook gently, uncovered, for 2 minutes. Remove from the heat, slightly mash the potato and peas, then add the cashews, mix well and season with salt.

2 To make the pastry, put the flour in a bowl and rub in the butter finely. Mix in the milk to form a dough. Knead lightly and divide into 6 portions. Form each into a ball and roll out on a lightly floured surface to an 18 cm/ 7 inch round. Cut each one in half.

3 Divide the filling equally between each semi-circle of pastry, spreading it out to within 5 mm/1/4 inch of the edges. Brush the edges of pastry all the way round with water and fold over to form triangular shapes, sealing the edges well together to enclose the filling completely.

4 One-third fill a large, deep frying pan (skillet) with oil and heat to 180°C/350°F or until hot enough to brown a cube of bread in 30 seconds. Fry the samosas, a few at a time, turning frequently until golden brown. Drain on paper towels and keep warm while cooking the remainder in the same way. Garnish with coriander (cilantro) sprigs and serve hot.

STEP 2

STEP 3

STEP 4

CHAPTER SEVEN

Main Dishes

❦

India has long stood as the undisputed centre of vegetarianism. This is partly due to religious reasons (Hindus are forbidden meat), and partly due to economic factors. The vegetarian dishes they eat therefore supply all the proteins, vitamins and minerals that the human body needs.

The Indians make great use of and show creative flair with their staples of rice, lentils, fruit, nuts, eggs, milk, pulses and vegetables to make a seemingly endless array of dishes from biryanis and curries to pilaus and paneers that delight the appetite.

Such basic foodstuffs are used to create spicy, wholesome curries; stuffed vegetable treats using aubergines and potatoes; rice and vegetable pilaus with crunchy nut crowns; and nut and lentil 'meatballs' better known as koftas. Mixed and matched with flavoursome rice, lentil, vegetable and bread accompaniments, they make a nutritious feast for the vegetarian.

Opposite: *Ploughing a rice paddy with the help of water buffaloes, near Madras.*

BROWN RICE WITH FRUIT & NUTS

*Here is a tasty and filling rice dish that is nice and spicy. It includes
fruits for a refreshing flavour and toasted nuts for an
interesting crunchy texture.*

STEP 1

STEP 2

STEP 3

STEP 4

SERVES 4–6

4 tbsp vegetable ghee or oil
1 large onion, chopped
2 garlic cloves, crushed
2.5 cm/1 inch piece ginger root, chopped
1 tsp chilli powder
1 tsp cumin seeds
1 tbsp mild or medium curry powder or
    paste
300 g/10 oz/1½ cups brown rice
900 ml/1½ pints/3½ cups boiling vegetable
    stock
425 g/14 oz can chopped tomatoes
175 g/6 oz ready-soaked dried apricots or
    peaches, cut into slivers
1 red (bell) pepper, diced
90 g/3 oz frozen peas
1–2 small, slightly green bananas
60–90g/2–3 oz/⅓–½ cup toasted nuts
    (a mixture of almonds, cashews and pine
    kernels (nuts) or hazelnuts)
salt and pepper
sprigs of fresh coriander (cilantro), to
    garnish

1 Heat the ghee or oil in a large
saucepan, add the onion and fry
gently for 3 minutes. Stir in the garlic,
ginger, spices and rice and cook gently
for 2 minutes, stirring all the time until
the rice is coated in the spiced oil.

2 Pour in the boiling stock and
canned tomatoes and season with
salt and pepper to taste. Bring to the boil,
then reduce the heat, cover and simmer
gently for 40 minutes or until the rice is
almost cooked and most of the liquid is
absorbed.

3 Add the slivered apricots or
peaches, diced red (bell) pepper and
peas. Cover and continue cooking for 10
minutes. Remove from the heat and
allow to stand for 5 minutes without
uncovering.

4 Peel and slice the bananas.
Uncover the rice mixture and fork
through to mix the ingredients together.
Add the toasted nuts and sliced banana
and toss lightly. Transfer to a warm
serving platter and garnish with
coriander (cilantro) sprigs. Serve hot.

BROWN RICE

Brown rice has a delicious nutty flavour
and a more chewy texture than white rice
and because the germ of the grain is
retained, it also contains larger amounts
of vitamins, minerals and protein. Brown
rice takes longer to cook than white rice.

MUTTAR PANEER

Paneer is a delicious fresh, soft cheese frequently used in Indian cooking. It is easily made at home, but remember to make it the day before required.

STEP 1

SERVES 6

150 ml/¼ pint/⅔ cup vegetable oil
2 onions, chopped
2 garlic cloves, crushed
2.5 cm/1 inch piece ginger root, chopped
1 tsp garam masala
1 tsp ground turmeric
1 tsp chilli powder
500 g/1 lb frozen peas
250 g/8 oz can chopped tomatoes
125 ml/4 fl oz/½ cup vegetable stock
salt and freshly ground black pepper
2 tbsp chopped fresh coriander

PANEER:
2.5 litres/4 pints/10 cups pasteurized full cream milk
5 tbsp lemon juice
1 garlic clove, crushed (optional)
1 tbsp chopped fresh coriander (cilantro) (optional)

1 To make the paneer, bring the milk to a rolling boil in a large saucepan. Remove from the heat and stir in the lemon juice. Return to the heat for about 1 minute until the curds and whey separate. Remove from the heat. Line a colander with double thickness muslin (cheesecloth) and pour the mixture through the muslin (cheesecloth), adding the garlic and coriander (cilantro), if using. Squeeze all the liquid from the curds and leave to drain.

2 Transfer the curds to a dish, cover with a plate and weights and leave overnight in the refrigerator.

STEP 3

3 Cut the pressed paneer into small cubes. Heat the oil in a large frying pan, add the paneer cubes and fry until golden on all sides. Remove from the pan and drain on paper towels.

4 Pour off some of the oil, leaving about 4 tablespoons in the pan. Add the onions, garlic and ginger and fry gently for about 5 minutes, stirring frequently. Stir in the spices and fry gently for 2 minutes. Add the peas, tomatoes and stock and season with salt and pepper. Cover and simmer for 10 minutes, stirring occasionally, until the onion is tender.

STEP 4

5 Add the fried paneer cubes and cook for a further 5 minutes. Taste and adjust the seasoning, if necessary. Serve at once.

STEP 5

STEP 2

STEP 3

STEP 4

STEP 5

SPLIT PEAS WITH VEGETABLES

*Here is a simple, yet nourishing and flavourful way of cooking yellow
split peas. Vary the selection of vegetables and spices according
to personal preferences.*

SERVES 4–5

250 g/ 8 oz/ 1 cup dried yellow split peas
1.25 litres/ 2¼ pints/ 5 cups cold water
½ tsp ground turmeric (optional)
500g/ 1 lb new potatoes
75 ml/ 3 fl oz/ 5 tbsp vegetable oil
2 onions, chopped coarsely
175 g/ 6 oz button mushrooms
1 tsp ground coriander
1 tsp ground cumin
1 tsp chilli powder
1 tsp garam masala
450 ml/ ¾ pint/ 1¾ cups vegetable stock
½ cauliflower, broken into florets
90 g/ 3 oz frozen peas
175 g/ 6 oz cherry tomatoes, halved
salt and pepper
sprigs of fresh mint to garnish

1 Place the split peas in a bowl, add
the cold water and leave to soak for
at least 4 hours or overnight.

2 Place the peas and the soaking
liquid in a fairly large saucepan,
stir in the turmeric, if using, and bring to
the boil. Skim off any surface scum, half-
cover the pan with a lid and simmer
gently for 20 minutes or until the peas
are tender and almost dry. Remove the
pan from the heat and reserve.

3 Meanwhile, cut the potatoes into
5 mm/ ¼ inch thick slices. Heat the
oil in a flameproof casserole, add the
onions, potatoes and mushrooms and
cook gently for 5 minutes, stirring
frequently. Stir in the spices and fry
gently for 1 minute, then add salt and
pepper to taste, the stock and cauliflower
florets.

4 Cover and simmer gently for 25
minutes or until the potato is
tender, stirring occasionally. Add the
split peas (and any of the cooking liquid)
and the frozen peas. Bring to the boil,
cover and continue cooking for 5
minutes.

5 Stir in the halved cherry tomatoes
and cook for 2 minutes. Taste and
adjust the seasoning, if necessary. Serve
hot, garnished with mint sprigs.

VARIATION

Chana dal (popular with vegetarians
because of its high protein content) may
be used instead of yellow split peas, if
preferred. Chana dal is similar to yellow
split peas, although the grains are smaller
and the flavour sweeter.

STUFFED AUBERGINES (EGGPLANT)

These are delicious served hot or cold, topped with natural yogurt or cucumber raita.

STEP 1

SERVES 6

250 g/8 oz/1¹/₃ cup continental lentils
900 ml/1¹/₂ pints/3³/₄ cups water
2 garlic cloves, crushed
3 well-shaped aubergines (eggplants)
150 ml/¹/₄ pint/²/₃ cup vegetable oil
2 onions, chopped
4 tomatoes, chopped
2 tsp cumin seeds
1 tsp ground cinnamon
2 tbsp mild curry paste
1 tsp minced chilli (from a jar)
2 tbsp chopped fresh mint
salt and pepper
sprigs of fresh mint to garnish

TO SERVE:
natural yogurt
chilli powder

1 Rinse the lentils under cold running water. Drain and place in a saucepan with the water and garlic. Cover and simmer for 30 minutes.

2 Cook the aubergines (eggplants) in a saucepan of boiling water for 5 minutes. Drain, then plunge into cold water for 5 minutes. Drain again. Cut in half lengthways. Scoop out most of the flesh and reserve, leaving a 1 cm/¹/₂ inch thick border to form a shell.

STEP 2

3 Place the aubergine (eggplant) shells in a shallow greased ovenproof dish, brush with a little oil and sprinkle with salt and pepper. Cook in a preheated oven at 180°C/350°F/Gas Mark 4 for 10 minutes. Meanwhile, heat half the remaining oil in a frying pan, add the onions and tomatoes and fry gently for 5 minutes. Chop the reserved aubergine (eggplant) flesh, add to the pan with the spices and cook gently for 5 minutes. Season with salt.

STEP 3

4 Stir in the lentils, most of the remaining oil, reserving a little for later, and the mint. Spoon the mixture into the shells. Drizzle with the remaining oil and bake for 15 minutes. Serve hot or cold topped with a spoonful of natural yogurt, sprinkled with chilli powder and garnished with mint sprigs.

AUBERGINES (EGGPLANTS)

Choose nice plump aubergines (eggplant) rather than thin tapering ones as these retain their shape better when filled and baked with a stuffing.

STEP 4

STEP 1

STEP 1

STEP 2

STEP 3

LENTIL & VEGETABLE BIRYANI

A delicious mix of vegetables, basmati rice and continental lentils produces a wholesome and nutritious dish.

SERVES 6

125 g/4 oz/²/₃ cup continental lentils
4 tbsp vegetable ghee or oil
2 onions, quartered and sliced
2 garlic cloves, crushed
2.5 cm/1 inch piece ginger root, chopped
1 tsp ground turmeric
¹/₂ tsp chilli powder
1 tsp ground coriander
2 tsp ground cumin
3 tomatoes, skinned and chopped
1 aubergine (eggplant), trimmed and cut
   into 1 cm/¹/₂ inch pieces
1.75 litres/2¹/₂ pints/6¹/₄ cups boiling
   vegetable stock
1 red or green (bell) pepper, diced
350 g/12 oz/1³/₄ cups basmati rice
125 g/4 oz/1 cup French (green) beans,
   halved
250 g/8 oz/1¹/₃ cups cauliflower florets
125 g/4 oz/1¹/₂ mushrooms, wiped and
   sliced or quartered
60 g/2 oz/¹/₂ cup unsalted cashews
3 hard-boiled (hard-cooked) eggs
sprigs of fresh coriander (cilantro) to
   garnish

1 Rinse the lentils under cold running water and drain. Heat the ghee or oil in a saucepan, add the onions and fry gently for 2 minutes. Stir in the garlic, ginger and spices and fry gently for 1 minute, stirring frequently. Add the lentils, tomatoes, aubergine (eggplant) and 600 ml/1 pint/2¹/₂ cups of the stock, mix well, then cover and simmer gently for 20 minutes. Add the red or green (bell) pepper and cook for a further 10 minutes or until the lentils are tender and all the liquid has been absorbed.

2 Meanwhile, place the rice in a sieve (strainer) and rinse under cold running water until the water runs clear. Drain and place in another pan with the remaining stock. Bring to the boil, add the French (green) beans, cauliflower and mushrooms, then cover and cook gently for 15 minutes or until rice and vegetables are tender. Remove from the heat and leave, covered, for 10 minutes.

3 Add the lentil mixture and the cashews to the cooked rice and mix lightly together. Pile onto a warm serving platter, top with wedges of hard-boiled (hard-cooked) egg and garnish with coriander (cilantro) sprigs.

STEP 1

STEP 2

STEP 3

STEP 3

JACKET POTATOES WITH BEANS

Baked jacket potatoes, topped with a tasty mixture of beans in a spicy sauce, provide a deliciously filling, high-fibre dish.

SERVES 6

6 large potatoes (for baking)
4 tbsp vegetable ghee or oil
1 large onion, chopped
2 garlic cloves, crushed
1 tsp ground turmeric
1 tbsp cumin seeds
2 tbsp mild or medium curry paste
350 g/12 oz cherry tomatoes
425 g/14 oz can black-eye beans (peas), drained and rinsed
425 g/14 oz can red kidney beans, drained and rinsed
1 tbsp lemon juice
2 tbsp tomato purée (paste)
150 ml/¼ pint/⅔ cup water
2 tbsp chopped fresh mint or coriander (cilantro)
salt and pepper
sprigs of fresh mint to garnish

1 Wash and scrub the potatoes and prick several times with a fork. Cook in a preheated oven at 200°C/400°F/Gas Mark 6 for 1–1¼ hours or until the potatoes feel soft.

2 About 20 minutes before the end of cooking time, prepare the topping. Heat the ghee or oil in a saucepan, add the onion and cook gently for 5 minutes, stirring frequently. Add the garlic, turmeric, cumin seeds and curry paste and cook gently for 1 minute. Stir in the tomatoes, black-eye beans (peas) and red kidney beans, lemon juice, tomato purée (paste), water and chopped mint or coriander (cilantro). Season with salt and pepper, then cover and cook gently for 10 minutes, stirring frequently.

3 When the potatoes are cooked, cut a cross in the top and squeeze gently to open out. Mash the flesh lightly with a fork. Spoon the prepared bean mixture on top, garnish with mint sprigs and serve.

VARIATION

Instead of cutting a cross in the potatoes, cut them lengthways in half. If there is any remaining filling, spoon it around the potatoes.

STEP 1

STEP 2

STEP 3

STEP 4

SPINACH & AUBERGINE (EGGPLANT)

This interesting combination of lentils and spiced vegetables is delicious served with parathas, chapatis or naan bread, plus a bowl of natural yogurt.

SERVES 4

250 g/8 oz/1 cup split red lentils
700 ml/1¼ pints/3 cups water
1 onion
1 aubergine (eggplant)
1 red (bell) pepper
2 courgettes (zucchini)
125 g/4 oz mushrooms
250 g/8 oz leaf spinach
4 tbsp vegetable ghee or oil
1 fresh green chilli, deseeded and chopped, or
    use 1 tsp minced chilli (from a jar)
1 tsp ground cumin
1 tsp ground coriander
2.5 cm/1 inch piece ginger root, chopped
150 ml/¼ pint/⅔ cup vegetable stock
salt

1 Wash the lentils and place in a saucepan with the water. Cover and simmer for 15 minutes until the lentils are soft but still whole.

2 Meanwhile, peel, quarter and slice the onion. Trim leaf end from the aubergine (eggplant) and cut into 1 cm/½ inch pieces. Remove stalk end and seeds from the (bell) pepper and cut into 1 cm/½ inch pieces. Trim and cut courgettes (zucchini) into 1 cm/½ inch thick slices. Thickly slice the mushrooms.

Discard coarse stalks from spinach leaves and wash spinach well.

3 Heat the ghee or oil in a large saucepan, add the onion and red (bell) pepper and fry gently for 3 minutes, stirring frequently. Stir in the aubergine (eggplant), courgettes (zucchini), mushrooms, chilli, spices and ginger and fry gently for 1 minute. Add the spinach and stock and season with salt to taste.

4 Stir and turn until the spinach leaves wilt down. Cover and simmer for 10 minutes or until the vegetables are just tender. Make a border of the lentils on a warm serving plate and spoon the vegetable mixture into the centre. (The lentils may be stirred into the vegetable mixture, instead of being used as a border, if wished.)

SPINACH

Wash the spinach thoroughly in several changes of cold water as it can be gritty. Drain well and shake off excess water from leaves before adding to the pan.

STEP 2

STEP 3

STEP 4

STEP 5

VEGETABLE, NUT & LENTIL KOFTAS

The mixture here is shaped into golf-ball shapes and baked in the oven with a sprinkling of aromatic garam masala. Delicious served hot (or cold) with a yogurt dressing and chapatis.

SERVES 4–5

6 tbsp vegetable ghee or oil
1 onion, chopped finely
2 carrots, chopped finely
2 celery sticks, chopped finely
2 garlic cloves, crushed
1 fresh green chilli, deseeded and chopped
    finely
1¹/₂ tbsp curry powder or paste
250 g/8 oz/1¹/₄ cups split red lentils
600 ml/1 pint/2¹/₂ cups vegetable stock
2 tbsp tomato purée (paste)
125 g/4 oz/2 cups fresh wholemeal
    (wholewheat) breadcrumbs
90 g/3 oz/³/₄ cup unsalted cashews, chopped
    finely
2 tbsp chopped fresh coriander (cilantro) or
    parsley
1 egg, beaten
salt and pepper
garam masala, for sprinkling

YOGURT DRESSING:
250 g/8 oz natural yogurt
1–2 tbsp chopped fresh coriander (cilantro)
1–2 tbsp mango chutney, chopped if
    necessary
coriander (cilantro) sprigs to garnish

1 Heat 4 tablespoons of ghee or oil in a large saucepan and gently fry the onion, carrots, celery, garlic and chilli for 5 minutes, stirring frequently. Add the curry powder or paste and the lentils and cook gently for 1 minute, stirring.

2 Add the stock and tomato purée (paste) and bring to the boil. Reduce the heat, cover and simmer for 20 minutes or until the lentils are tender and all the liquid is absorbed.

3 Remove from the heat and cool slightly. Add the breadcrumbs, nuts, coriander (cilantro), egg and seasoning to taste. Mix well and leave to cool. Using 2 spoons, shape into rounds about the size of golf balls.

4 Place the balls on a greased baking sheet (cookie sheet), drizzle with the remaining oil and sprinkle with a little garam masala, to taste. Cook in a preheated oven at 180C/350F/Gas Mark 4 for 15–20 minutes or until piping hot and lightly golden.

5 Meanwhile, make the yogurt dressing. Mix all the ingredients together in a bowl. Garnish with coriander (cilantro) sprigs. Serve the koftas hot with the yogurt dressing.

SPICED CHICK-PEAS (GARBANZO BEANS)

Canned chick-peas (garbanzo beans), widely available from supermarkets, are used in this dish, but you could use black-eye beans (peas) if you prefer. Omit the chillies for a less fiery flavour.

STEP 1

SERVES 4

1 large aubergine (eggplant)
2 courgettes (zucchini)
6 tbsp vegetable ghee or oil
1 large onion, quartered and sliced
2 garlic cloves, crushed
1–2 fresh green chillies, deseeded and
   chopped, or use 1–2 tsp minced chilli
   (from a jar)
2 tsp ground coriander
2 tsp cumin seeds
1 tsp ground turmeric
1 tsp garam masala
425 g/14 oz can chopped tomatoes
300 ml/½ pint/1¼ cups vegetable stock or
   water
425 g/14 oz can chick-peas (garbanzo
   beans), drained and rinsed
2 tbsp chopped fresh mint
150 ml/¼ pint/⅔ cup double (heavy)
   cream
salt and pepper

2 Stir in the spices and cook for 30 seconds. Add the tomatoes, stock and salt and pepper to taste and cook for 10 minutes.

3 Add the chick-peas (garbanzo beans) to the pan and continue cooking for a further 5 minutes. Stir in the mint and cream and reheat gently. Taste and adjust the seasoning, if necessary. Serve hot with plain or pilau rice, or with parathas, if preferred.

STEP 1

STEP 2

1 Trim the leaf end off aubergine (eggplant) and cut into cubes. Trim and slice the courgettes (zucchini). Heat the ghee or oil in a saucepan and gently fry the aubergine (eggplant), courgettes (zucchini), onion, garlic and chillies for about 5 minutes, stirring frequently and adding a little more oil if necessary.

YOGURT

You could use natural yogurt instead of cream in this dish, in which case first blend it with ½ teaspoon cornflour (cornstarch) before adding to the pan and heating gently, stirring constantly. The cornflour (cornstarch) helps stabilize the yogurt to prevent it separating during heating.

STEP 3

STEP 1

STEP 2

STEP 3

STEP 4

VEGETABLE CURRY

*This colourful and interesting mixture of vegetables, cooked in a spicy
sauce, is excellent served with rice and naan bread. Vary the vegetables
according to personal preferences.*

SERVES 4

250 g/8 oz turnips or swede
1 aubergine (eggplant)
250 g/8 oz cauliflower
250 g/8 oz button mushrooms
350 g/12 oz new potatoes
1 large onion
250 g/8 oz carrots
6 tbsp vegetable ghee or oil
2 garlic cloves, crushed
5 cm/2 inch piece ginger root, chopped
1–2 fresh green chillies, deseeded and
    chopped
1 tbsp paprika
2 tsp ground coriander
1 tbsp mild or medium curry powder or
    paste
450 ml/³/₄ pint/1³/₄ cups vegetable stock
425 g/14 oz can chopped tomatoes
1 green (bell) pepper, sliced
1 tbsp cornflour (cornstarch)
150 ml/¹/₄ pint/²/₃ cup coconut milk
2–3 tbsp ground almonds
salt
coriander (cilantro) sprigs to garnish

1 Cut the turnips or swede,
aubergine (eggplant) and potatoes
into 1 cm/¹/₂ inch cubes. Divide the
cauliflower into small florets. Leave the
mushrooms and potatoes whole, or slice

thickly. Slice the onion and carrots.

2 Heat the ghee or oil in a large
saucepan, add the onion, carrots,
turnip, potatoes and cauliflower and
cook gently for 3 minutes, stirring. Add
the garlic, ginger, chilli and spices and
cook for 1 minute, stirring.

3 Add the stock, tomatoes, aubergine
(eggplant) and mushrooms and
season with salt. Cover and simmer
gently for about 30 minutes or until
tender, stirring occasionally. Add the
green (bell) pepper, cover and continue
cooking for a further 5 minutes.

4 Blend the cornflour (cornstarch)
with the coconut milk and stir into
the mixture. Add the ground almonds
and simmer for 2 minutes, stirring.
Adjust the seasoning, if necessary. Serve
hot, garnished with coriander (cilantro).

GROUND ALMONDS

The ground almonds used in this dish not
only help to thicken the sauce but also add
richness and flavour to it. For a less fiery
flavour, reduce or omit the amount of
chilli used.

CHAPTER EIGHT

Accompaniments

❧

Bread accompanies nearly every Indian meal in the form of parathas, which are basically fried chapatis; naan, or leavened baked bread; crisp and crunchy poppadoms, flavoured or plain; and pooris, small rounds of deep-fried bread that are sometimes stuffed with savoury ingredients.

Vegetable accompaniments come in all guises: as mixed curried dishes; as fritters, tasty with a spoonful of relish; and as bhajis, which are basically fried and spiced vegetables. They all contribute to give an Indian meal flavour and texture as well as extra nourishment.

Needless to say rice is a staple food and, in the south particularly, is served as a matter of course with virtually every meal. Experiment by cooking it in a little coconut milk with just a pinch of spice such as garam masala to liven up plain boiled rice. Also consider serving spiced potatoes and cooked lentils as an alternative to rice – they make a welcome change and provide good nutrition.

Opposite: *An Indian market stall sells a colourful array of herbs and spices.*

AUBERGINE (EGGPLANT) IN SAFFRON

Here is a quick and simple, delicately spiced and delicious way to cook aubergines (eggplant).

STEP 1

SERVES 4

a good pinch of saffron strands, finely crushed
1 tbsp boiling water
1 large aubergine (eggplant)
3 tbsp vegetable oil
1 large onion, chopped coarsely
2 garlic cloves, crushed
2.5 cm/1 inch piece ginger root, chopped
1½ tbsp mild or medium curry paste
1 tsp cumin seeds
150 ml/¼ pint/⅔ cup double (heavy) cream
150 ml/¼ pint/⅔ cup strained thick yogurt
2 tbsp mango chutney, chopped if necessary
salt and pepper
coriander (cilantro) leaves to garnish

1 Place the saffron in a small bowl, add the boiling water and leave to infuse for 5 minutes. Trim the leaf end off the aubergine (eggplant), cut lengthways into quarters, then into 1 cm/½ inch thick slices.

2 Heat the oil in a large frying pan (skillet), add the onion and cook gently for 3 minutes. Stir in the aubergine (eggplant), garlic, ginger, curry paste and cumin and cook gently for 3 minutes.

3 Stir in the saffron water, cream, yogurt and chutney and cook gently for 8–10 minutes, stirring frequently, until the aubergine (eggplant) is cooked through and tender. Season with salt and pepper to taste, garnish with coriander (cilantro) leaves and serve hot.

STEP 1

YOGURT

You will find that yogurt adds a creamy texture and pleasant tartness to this sauce. If you are worried about it curdling on heating, add a tablespoonful at a time and stir it in well before adding another. A little cornflour (cornstarch) blended with the yogurt before cooking, also helps prevent it from separating when heated.

STEP 2

STEP 3

STEP 1

STEP 1

STEP 2

STEP 3

SPINACH & CAULIFLOWER BHAJI

*This excellent vegetable dish goes well with most Indian food –
and it is simple and quick-cooking, too.*

SERVES 4

1 cauliflower
500 g/1 lb fresh spinach
4 tbsp vegetable ghee or oil
2 large onions, chopped coarsely
2 garlic cloves, crushed
2.5 cm/1 inch piece ginger root, chopped
1¼ tsp chilli powder, or to taste
1 tsp ground cumin
1 tsp ground turmeric
2 tsp ground coriander
425 g/14 oz can chopped tomatoes
300 ml/½ pint/1¼ cups vegetable stock
salt and pepper

1 Divide the cauliflower into small florets, discarding the hard central stalk. Trim the stalks from the spinach leaves. Heat the ghee or oil in a large saucepan, add the onions and cauliflower florets and fry the vegetables gently for about 3 minutes, stirring frequently.

2 Add the garlic, ginger and spices and cook gently for 1 minute. Stir in the tomatoes and the stock and season with salt and pepper. Bring to the boil, cover, reduce the heat and simmer gently for 8 minutes.

3 Add the spinach to the pan, stirring and turning to wilt the leaves. Cover and simmer gently for about 8–10 minutes, stirring frequently until the spinach has wilted and the cauliflower is tender. Serve hot.

SPINACH

You may prefer to use frozen spinach in this recipe, in which case you require 250 g/8 oz frozen leaf spinach which must be defrosted and well drained before adding to the mixture and heating through.

FRIED SPICED POTATOES

Deliciously good and a super accompaniment to almost any main course dish, though rather high in calories!

STEP 1

SERVES 4–6

2 onions, quartered
5 cm/2 inch piece ginger root, chopped
2 garlic cloves
2–3 tbsp mild or medium curry paste
4 tbsp water
750 g/1½ lb new potatoes
vegetable oil, for deep frying
3 tbsp vegetable ghee or oil
150 ml/¼ pint/⅔ cup strained thick yogurt
150 ml/¼ pint/⅔ cup double (heavy) cream
3 tbsp chopped fresh mint
salt and pepper
½ bunch spring onions (scallions), chopped, to garnish

STEP 2

1 Place the onions, ginger, garlic, curry paste and water in a blender or food processor and process until smooth, scraping down the sides of machine and blending again, if necessary. Alternatively, chop the onions, ginger and garlic very finely and mix with the curry paste and water.

STEP 3

2 Cut the potatoes into quarters – the pieces need to be about 2.5 cm/ 1 inch in size – and pat dry with paper towels. Heat the oil in a deep-fat fryer to 180°C/350°F or until hot enough to brown a cube of bread in 30 seconds. Fry the potatoes, in batches, for about 5 minutes or until golden brown, turning frequently. Remove from the pan and drain on paper towels.

STEP 4

3 Heat the ghee or oil in a large frying pan (skillet), add the curry and onion mixture and fry gently for 2 minutes, stirring all the time. Add the yogurt, cream and 2 tablespoons of mint and mix well.

4 Add the fried potatoes and stir until coated in the sauce. Cook for a further 5–7 minutes or until heated through and sauce has thickened, stirring frequently. Season with salt and pepper to taste and sprinkle with the remaining mint and sliced spring onions (scallions). Serve immediately.

STEP 1

STEP 2

STEP 3

STEP 4

SWEET HOT CARROTS & BEANS

Take care not to overcook the vegetables in this tasty dish – they are definitely at their best served tender-crisp. Remember to discard the whole dried chillies before serving the dish.

SERVES 4

500 g/ 1 lb young carrots
250 g/8 oz French (green) beans
1 bunch spring onions (scallions)
4 tbsp vegetable ghee or oil
1 tsp ground cumin
1 tsp ground coriander
3 cardamom pods, split and seeds removed
2 whole dried red chillies
2 garlic cloves, peeled and crushed
1–2 tsp clear honey, to taste
1 tsp lemon or lime juice
60 g/2 oz/$\frac{1}{2}$ cup unsalted, toasted cashews
1 tbsp chopped fresh coriander (cilantro) or
  parsley
salt and pepper
slices of lemon or lime to serve

1 Cut the carrots lengthways into quarters and then in half crossways if very long. Top and tail the beans. Cut the spring onions (scallions) into 5 cm/2 inch pieces. Cook the carrots and beans in a saucepan containing a little boiling, salted water for 5–6 minutes until just tender. Drain well.

2 Heat the ghee or oil in a large frying pan (skillet), add the spring onions (scallions), carrots, beans, cumin, coriander, cardamom seeds and whole dried chillies. Cook gently for 2 minutes, stirring frequently.

3 Stir in the garlic, honey and lemon or lime juice and continue cooking for a further 2 minutes, stirring occasionally. Season to taste with salt and pepper. Remove and discard the whole chillies.

4 Sprinkle the vegetables with the toasted cashews and chopped coriander (cilantro) and mix together lightly. Serve immediately, with slices of lemon or lime.

CARROTS

If the carrots are very slender it may not be necessary to cut them into quarters, simply trim the leafy ends, scrub well and cook in the boiling, salted water for a minute or two before adding the French (green) beans to ensure all the vegetables cook evenly.

STARTERS

•

FISH DISHES

•

MEAT & POULTRY DISHES

•

ACCOMPANIMENTS

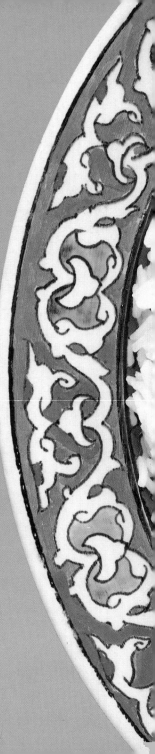

3

**QUICK &
EASY DISHES**

CHAPTER NINE

Starters

❀

Whether you are planning a full-scale dinner party, an informal buffet or a nourishing family meal, don't forget to include a starter or a few appetizers to tempt the tastebuds at the start of the meal. Dishes such as Spicy Chicken Tikka, Prawn (Shrimp) Pooris or Lamb & Tomato Koftas are an ideal way to start a meal. Use hot spices cautiously in such palate-enticing dishes, and serve with a cooling sauce such as Cucumber Raita.

Alternatively, do as the Indians do and serve a selection of snack foods like pakoras before the main meal – they are perfect finger food to serve with drinks.

Opposite: *A bustling scene at Crawford Market in Bombay.*

STEP 1

STEP 2

STEP 4

STEP 5

PRAWN (SHRIMP) POORIS

Tiger prawns (shrimp) are especially good cooked this way, although the less expensive, smaller peeled prawns (shrimp) may be used instead.

SERVES 6

POORIS:
60 g/2 oz/¹/₂ cup plain (all-purpose) wholemeal (wholewheat) flour
60 g/2 oz/¹/₂ cup plain (all-purpose) white flour
1 tbsp ghee or vegetable oil
2 good pinches of salt
75 ml/3 fl oz/5 tbsp hot water

TOPPING:
250 g/8 oz fresh spinach
4 tbsp ghee or vegetable oil, plus extra oil for shallow frying
1 onion, chopped
1 garlic clove, crushed
¹/₂–1 tsp minced chilli (from a jar)
1–1¹/₂ tbsp medium curry paste, to taste
250 g/8 oz can chopped tomatoes
150 ml/¹/₄ pint/²/₃ cup coconut milk
250 g/8 oz peeled tiger prawns (shrimp)
salt

1 To make the pooris, put the flours in a bowl and make a well in the centre. Add the ghee or oil, salt and hot water and mix to form a dough. Leave to stand for 1 hour.

2 Meanwhile, prepare the topping. Cut the spinach crossways into wide strips – do this by making bundles of leaves and slicing with a sharp knife.

3 Heat the ghee or oil in a frying pan (skillet), add the onion, garlic, chilli and spinach and cook gently for 4 minutes, shaking the pan and stirring frequently. Add the curry paste, tomatoes and coconut milk and simmer for 10 minutes, stirring occasionally. Remove from the heat, stir in the prawns (shrimp) and season with salt to taste.

4 Knead the dough well on a floured surface, divide into 6 pieces and shape into 6 balls. Roll out each one to a 12 cm/5 inch round. Heat about 2.5 cm/1 inch oil in a deep frying pan (skillet) until smoking hot. Take one poori at a time, lower into the hot oil and cook for 10–15 seconds on each side until puffed up and golden. Remove the poori with a slotted spoon, drain on paper towels and keep warm while cooking the remainder in the same way.

5 Reheat the prawn (shrimp) mixture. Arrange a poori on each serving plate and spoon the prawn (shrimp) mixture on to each one. Serve immediately.

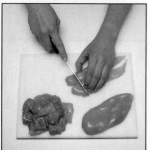

STEP 1

STEP 2

STEP 3

STEP 4

SPICY CHICKEN TIKKA

*Arrange these tasty kebabs on a bed of finely shredded crisp lettuce,
slivered onion and grated eating apple drizzled with a little
lemon or lime juice.*

SERVES 6

500 g / 1 lb boneless chicken breasts, skinned
1¹/₂ tbsp tikka paste (from a jar)
6 tbsp strained thick yogurt
1 tbsp lemon juice
¹/₂ onion, chopped finely
*1¹/₂ tbsp chopped fresh chives or spring
     onion leaves*
1¹/₂ tbsp finely chopped ginger root
1–2 garlic cloves, crushed
1¹/₂ tbsp sesame seeds
2 tbsp vegetable oil
salt and pepper

1 Cut the chicken breasts into small
bite-sized pieces, place in a shallow
glass dish and season with salt and
pepper to taste.

2 In a small bowl, mix together the
remaining ingredients, except the
sesame seeds and oil, and pour over the
chicken. Mix well until all the chicken
pieces are coated, then cover and
refrigerate for at least 1 hour, or for
longer if possible.

3 Thread the chicken pieces onto 6
bamboo or metal skewers and
sprinkle with the sesame seeds.

4 Place on a rack in a grill (broiler)
pan and drizzle with the oil. Cook
under a hot grill (broiler) for about 15
minutes or until cooked through and
browned, turning frequently and
brushing with more oil, if necessary.
Serve hot.

HELPFUL HINTS

To prevent bamboo skewers charring
during cooking, soak them first in cold
water for 30 minutes before threading
with the chicken.

STEP 1

STEP 2

STEP 3

STEP 4

GARLICKY MUSHROOM PAKORAS

Whole mushrooms are dunked in a spiced garlicky batter and deep fried until golden. They are at their most delicious served hot and freshly cooked.

SERVES 6

175 g/6 oz/1½ cups gram flour
½ tsp salt
¼ tsp baking powder
1 tsp cumin seeds
½–1 tsp chilli powder, to taste
200 ml/7 fl oz/¾ cup water
2 garlic cloves, crushed
1 small onion, chopped finely
vegetable oil, for deep frying
500 g/1 lb button mushrooms
lemon wedges to serve
sprigs of fresh coriander (cilantro) to garnish

1 Put the gram flour, salt, baking powder, cumin and chilli powder into a bowl and mix well together. Make a well in the centre of the mixture and gradually stir in the water, mixing to form a batter.

2 Stir the crushed garlic and the chopped onion into the batter and leave the mixture to infuse for 10 minutes. One-third fill a deep-fat fryer or pan with vegetable oil and heat to 180°C/350°F or until hot enough to brown a cube of day-old bread in 30 seconds.

3 Meanwhile, mix the mushrooms into the batter, stirring to coat. Remove a few at a time and place them into the hot oil. Fry for about 2 minutes or until golden brown.

4 Remove from the pan with a slotted spoon and drain on paper towels while cooking the remainder in the same way. Serve hot with lemon wedges and garnished with coriander (cilantro) sprigs.

GRAM FLOUR

Gram flour (also known as besan flour) is a pale yellow flour made from chick-peas (garbanzo beans). It is now readily available from larger supermarkets as well as Indian food shops and some ethnic delicatessens. Gram flour is also used to make onion bhajis.

STEP 1

STEP 1

STEP 2

STEP 3

LAMB & TOMATO KOFTAS

*These little meatballs, served with a minty yogurt dressing, can be
prepared well in advance, ready to cook when required.*

SERVES 4

*250 g/8 oz finely minced lean lamb
1½ onions
1–2 garlic cloves, crushed
1 dried red chilli, finely chopped (optional)
2–3 tsp garam masala
2 tbsp chopped fresh mint
2 tsp lemon juice
2 tbsp vegetable oil
4 small tomatoes, quartered
salt
sprigs of fresh mint to garnish*

*YOGURT DRESSING:
150 ml/¼ pint/⅔ cup strained thick yogurt
5 cm/2 inch piece cucumber, grated
2 tbsp chopped fresh mint
½ tsp toasted cumin seeds (optional)*

1 Place the minced lamb in a bowl.
Finely chop 1 onion and add to the
bowl with the garlic and chilli, if using.
Stir in the garam masala, mint and
lemon juice and season well with salt.
Mix the ingredients well together. Divide
the mixture in half, then divide each half
into 10 equal portions and form each
into a small ball. Roll balls in the oil to
coat. Quarter the remaining onion half
and separate into layers.

2 Thread 5 of the balls, 4 tomato
quarters and some of the onion
layers onto each of 4 bamboo or metal
skewers. Brush the vegetables with the
remaining oil and cook under a hot grill
for about 10 minutes, turning frequently
until they are browned all over and
cooked through.

3 Meanwhile, prepare the yogurt
dressing. Mix the yogurt with the
cucumber, mint and toasted cumin
seeds, if using. Garnish the lamb koftas
with mint sprigs and serve hot with the
yogurt dressing.

SHAPING KOFTAS

It is important that the lamb is finely
minced and the onion finely chopped or
the mixture will not shape neatly and
easily into balls. The mixture could be
finely processed in a food processor, if
wished.

CHAPTER TEN

Fish Dishes

❦

At first glance, India may not be considered to be a great fish-eating nation, but there are some parts of it, notably Bengal and around Karachi, where fish is very popular and consequently plays a very important part in the diet. Indeed India has a coastline stretching for over 2,500 miles and with internal waters can supply over 2,000 varieties of fish!

Many fish and shellfish are simply grilled (broiled), whole or on skewers, after sprinkling with a few spices and brushing with mustard oil; others are fried whole or as fish and vegetable fritters; some with a firm, meaty texture, like cod, are curried in aromatic sauces and frequently flavoured with coconut. Countless others are baked, steamed, poached or roasted with that characteristic Indian flavour that is based on a masala of spices that enhances, but does not overwhelm, the delicate flavour of the fish.

Opposite: Pushkar Lake, Rajasthan. Both freshwater fish and seafood play a large part in the cooking styles of India.

STEP 1

STEP 1

STEP 2

STEP 3

PRAWNS (SHRIMP) & CHILLI SAUCE

Quick and easy to prepare and extremely good to eat. Use the large and succulent tiger prawns (shrimp) for special occasions.

SERVES 4

4 tbsp ghee or vegetable oil
1 onion, quartered and sliced
1 bunch spring onions (scallions), sliced
1 garlic clove, crushed
1–2 fresh green chillies, deseeded and
    chopped finely
2.5 cm/1 inch piece ginger root, chopped
    finely
1 tsp ground turmeric
1 tsp ground cumin
1 tsp ground coriander
1½ tsp curry powder or paste
425 g/14 oz can chopped tomatoes
150 ml/¼ pint/⅔ cup water
150 ml/¼ pint/⅔ cup double (heavy)
    cream
500 g/1 lb peeled prawns (shrimp)
1–2 tbsp chopped fresh coriander (cilantro)
salt
sprigs of fresh coriander (cilantro) sprigs to
    garnish

1 Heat the ghee or vegetable oil in a saucepan and fry the onions, garlic and chilli over a gentle heat for 3 minutes. Stir in the ginger, spices and curry powder or paste and cook very gently for a further 1 minute, stirring all the time.

2 Stir in the tomatoes and water and bring to the boil, stirring. Reduce the heat and simmer for 10 minutes, stirring occasionally.

3 Add the cream, mix well and simmer for 5 minutes, then add the prawns (shrimp) and coriander (cilantro) and season with salt to taste. Cook gently for 2–3 minutes. Taste and adjust the seasoning, if necessary. Serve garnished with coriander (cilantro) sprigs.

PREPARE AHEAD

This dish may be prepared in advance to the end of step 2. A few minutes before the dish is required for serving, reheat the mixture until simmering then follow the instructions given in step 3.

INDIAN GRILLED TROUT

Here is a deliciously simple way of preparing and cooking trout.
It is also good with nice fresh, plump mackerel.

STEP 1

SERVES 4

4 trout, about 250 g/8 oz each, cleaned
6 tbsp ghee or melted butter
1–2 garlic cloves, crushed
1 fresh green chilli, deseeded and chopped, or
    use 1 tsp minced chilli (from a jar)
2.5 cm/1 inch piece ginger root, chopped
    finely
1½ tsp cumin seeds
1 tsp garam masala
1 tsp ground cumin
finely grated rind of 1 lemon
juice of 2 lemons
salt

TO GARNISH:
sprigs of fresh coriander (cilantro)
lemon wedges

1 Using a sharp knife, carefully make 3 diagonal slashes (not too deep) on each side of the trout. Season the trout and place in a lightly greased grill (broiler) pan or baking sheet (cookie sheet).

2 Heat the ghee or butter in a small pan over a low heat, add the crushed garlic, chilli, chopped ginger and spices and cook very gently for 30 seconds, stirring. Remove the pan from

the heat and stir the lemon rind and juice into the mixture.

3 Spoon half the mixture over the trout and cook under a preheated moderately hot grill (broiler) for 5–8 minutes or until cooked on one side. Turn the fish over and spoon the remaining mixture over the fish and grill (broil) for a further 5–8 minutes, basting with the juices in pan during cooking.

4 Arrange the trout on a hot serving plate, spoon the pan juices over the fish and garnish with coriander (cilantro) sprigs and lemon wedges. Serve hot.

STEP 2

STEP 2

SLASHING THE TROUT

Take care when making the diagonal slashes on either side of the trout not to cut too deeply or you will cut into the bones and spoil the finished result.

STEP 3

SEAFOOD & AROMATIC RICE

One of those easy, delicious meals where the rice and fish are cooked together in one pan. The whole spices are not meant to be eaten: they are there to flavour the dish during cooking and are removed before serving.

STEP 1

SERVES 4

250 g/8 oz/1¼ cups basmati rice
2 tbsp ghee or vegetable oil
1 onion, chopped
1 garlic clove, crushed
1 tsp cumin seeds
½–1 tsp chilli powder
4 cloves
1 cinnamon stick or a piece of cassia bark
2 tsp curry paste
250 g/8 oz peeled prawns (shrimp)
500g/1 lb white fish fillets (such as monkfish, cod or haddock), skinned and boned and cut into bite-sized pieces
600 ml/1 pint/2½ cups boiling water
60 g/2 oz/⅓ cup frozen peas
60 g/2 oz/⅓ cup frozen sweetcorn
1–2 tbsp lime juice
2 tbsp toasted desiccated (shredded) coconut
salt and pepper

TO GARNISH:
sprigs of fresh coriander (cilantro)
lime slices

1 Place the rice in a sieve (strainer) and wash under cold running water until the water runs clear. Drain well. Heat the ghee or oil in a saucepan, add the onion, garlic, spices and curry paste and fry gently for 1 minute.

STEP 2

2 Stir in the rice and mix well until coated in the spiced oil. Add the prawns (shrimp) and white fish and season well with salt and pepper. Stir lightly, then pour in the boiling water.

3 Cover and cook gently for 10 minutes, without uncovering the pan. Add the peas and corn, cover and continue cooking for a further 8 minutes. Remove from the heat and allow to stand, still covered, for 10 minutes.

STEP 3

4 Uncover the pan, fluff up the rice with a fork and transfer to a warm serving platter. Sprinkle the dish with the lime juice and toasted coconut, and serve garnished with coriander (cilantro) sprigs and lime slices.

VARIATION

For yellow rice, add ½ teaspoon ground turmeric to the pan together with the other spices at step 1. Alternatively, to add flavour as well as colour to the dish, omit the turmeric and instead add 2 good pinches of toasted and crushed saffron strands.

STEP 4

STEP 1

STEP 2

STEP 3

STEP 3

INDIAN COD WITH TOMATOES

Quick and easy – cod steaks are cooked in a rich tomato and coconut sauce to produce tender, succulent results. You can, of course, use any firm white fish available instead of cod.

SERVES 4

3 tbsp vegetable oil
4 cod steaks, about 2.5 cm/1 inch thick
1 onion, finely chopped
2 garlic cloves, crushed
1 red (bell) pepper, chopped
1 tsp ground coriander
1 tsp ground cumin
1 tsp ground turmeric
$^{1}/_{2}$ tsp garam masala
425 g/14 oz can chopped tomatoes
150 ml/$^{1}/_{4}$ pint/$^{2}/_{3}$ cup coconut milk
1–2 tbsp chopped fresh coriander (cilantro)
   or parsley
salt and pepper

1 Heat the oil in a frying pan (skillet), add the fish steaks, season with salt and pepper and fry until browned on both sides (but not cooked through). Remove from the pan and reserve.

2 Add the onion, garlic, red (bell) pepper and spices and cook very gently for 2 minutes, stirring frequently. Add the tomatoes, bring to the boil and simmer for 5 minutes.

3 Add the fish steaks to the pan and simmer gently for 8 minutes or until the fish is cooked through. Remove from the pan and keep warm on a serving dish. Add the coconut milk and coriander (cilantro) to the pan and reheat gently. Spoon the sauce over the cod steaks and serve immediately.

VARIATIONS

The mixture may be flavoured with a tablespoonful of curry powder or curry paste (mild, medium or hot, according to personal preference) instead of the mixture of spices at step 2, if wished.

128

CHAPTER ELEVEN

Meat & Poultry Dishes

❈

Curries are, of course, the most famous of the Indian meat dishes, but there are many dishes, in a variety of styles, that are quick and easy to prepare. Consider stir-fries with a blend of Indian spices, skewered kebabs of meat and vegetables, vegetables stuffed with savoury meat and rice or lentil mixtures, risotto-style combinations of meat with rice, or meat roasted tandoori-style.

Even then there are differences and variations which give a typical national dish a distinctive regional flavour all of its own. South Indian curries, for example, are fierce and fiery, while North Kashmiri and Punjab meat dishes are mild and strongly flavoured with onion and garlic. Western or Goan dishes are slow-cooked, hot and thickened with coconut milk, whereas Eastern meat dishes rely upon spices like mustard, cumin and anise for their distinctive flavour and originality.

Opposite: Unloading supplies on the banks of the Ganges, in the holy city of Benares.

STEP 1

STEP 1

STEP 2

STEP 2

SPICY CHICKEN

This is a delicious combination of chick-peas (garbanzo beans) and chicken flavoured with fragrant spices. Using canned chick-peas (garbanzo beans) rather than the dried ones speeds up the cooking time.

SERVES 4

3 tbsp ghee or vegetable oil
8 small chicken portions, such as thighs or
 drumsticks
1 large onion, chopped
2 garlic cloves, crushed
1–2 fresh green chillies, deseeded and
 chopped, or use 1–2 tsp minced chilli
 (from a jar)
2 tsp ground cumin
2 tsp ground coriander
1 tsp garam masala
1 tsp ground turmeric
425 g/14 oz can chopped tomatoes
150 ml/¼ pint/⅔ cup water
1 tbsp chopped fresh mint
475 g/15 oz can chick-peas (garbanzo
 beans), drained and rinsed
salt
natural yogurt to serve (optional)
coriander (cilantro) sprigs to garnish

1 Heat the ghee or oil in a large frying pan (skillet) and fry the chicken pieces all over until sealed and lightly golden. Remove from the pan. Add the onion, garlic, chilli and spices and cook very gently for 2 minutes, stirring frequently.

2 Stir in the tomatoes, water, mint and chick-peas (garbanzo beans). Mix well, return the chicken portions to the pan, season with salt to taste, then cover and simmer gently for about 20 minutes or until the chicken is tender and cooked through.

3 Taste and adjust the seasoning if necessary, then garnish with the coriander (cilantro) and serve hot, drizzled with yogurt, if using.

VARIATIONS

Canned black-eyed beans and red kidney beans also make delicious additions to this spicy chicken dish. Be sure to drain the canned beans and to rinse them, if necessary, before adding to the pan.

AROMATIC CHICKEN & ALMONDS

Rich and delicious – enjoy the succulence of chicken cooked with yogurt, cream and ground almonds flavoured with aromatic garam masala.

STEP 1

SERVES 4

150 ml/¼ pint/²⁄₃ cup strained thick yogurt
½ tsp cornflour (cornstarch)
4 tbsp ghee or vegetable oil
4 skinless boneless chicken breasts
2 onions, sliced
1 garlic clove, crushed
2.5 cm/1 inch piece ginger root, chopped
1½ tbsp garam masala
½ tsp chilli powder
2 tsp medium curry paste
300 ml/½ pint/1¼ cups chicken stock
150 ml/¼ pint/²⁄₃ cup double (heavy)
   cream
60 g/2 oz/½ cup ground almonds
125 g/4 oz French (green) beans, halved
2 tbsp lemon juice
salt and pepper
toasted flaked (slivered) almonds to garnish
boiled rice to serve

1 Smoothly blend the yogurt in a small bowl with the cornflour (cornstarch). Heat the ghee or oil in a large flameproof casserole, add the chicken breasts and fry until golden all over. Remove the chicken from the casserole and reserve.

2 Add the onions, garlic and ginger to the casserole and fry gently for 3 minutes, then add the garam masala, chilli powder and curry paste and fry gently for 1 minute. Stir in the stock, yogurt and salt and pepper to taste and bring to the boil, stirring all the time.

STEP 2

3 Return the chicken breasts to the casserole, then cover and simmer gently for 25 minutes. Remove the chicken to a dish and keep warm.

4 Blend the cream with the ground almonds and add to the sauce, then stir in the green beans and lemon juice and boil vigorously for 1 minute, stirring all the time.

STEP 4

5 Return the chicken to the casserole, cover and cook gently for a further 10 minutes. Serve with rice and garnish with toasted flaked (slivered) almonds.

ALTERNATIVE

Chicken portions may be used instead of breasts, if preferred, and should be cooked for 10 minutes longer at step 3.

STEP 5

BEEF & MUSHROOM CURRY

Vary the meat here according to personal taste, using lean lamb or pork (leg or shoulder cuts are ideal) instead of beef. Omit the finishing touches in step 4, if wished.

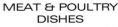

STEP 1

SERVES 4

750 g/1½ lb lean braising beef, trimmed
3 tbsp vegetable oil
2 onions, quartered and sliced
2 garlic cloves, crushed
2.5 cm/1 inch piece ginger root, chopped
2 fresh green chillies, deseeded and chopped, or use 1–2 tsp minced chilli (from a jar)
1½ tbsp medium curry paste
1 tsp ground coriander
175–250 g/6–8 oz mushrooms, thickly sliced
900 ml/1½ pints/3½ cups stock or water
3 tomatoes, chopped
½–1 tsp salt
60 g/2 oz creamed coconut, chopped
2 tbsp ground almonds

TO FINISH:
2 tbsp vegetable oil
1 red or green (bell) pepper, cut into thin strips
6 spring onions (scallions), sliced
1 tsp cumin seeds

1 Cut the beef into small bite-sized cubes. Heat the oil in a saucepan, add the beef and fry until sealed, stirring frequently. Remove from the pan.

2 Add the onions, garlic, ginger, chillies, curry paste and coriander to the pan and cook gently for 2 minutes. Stir in the mushrooms, stock and tomatoes and season with salt to taste. Return the beef to the pan, then cover and simmer very gently for 1¼–1½ hours or until beef is tender.

3 Stir the chopped creamed coconut and ground almonds into the curry, then cover the pan and cook gently for 3 minutes.

4 Meanwhile, heat the remaining oil in a frying pan (skillet), add the (bell) pepper strips and spring onion (scallion) slices and fry gently until glistening and tender-crisp. Stir in the cumin seeds and fry gently for 30 seconds, then spoon the mixture over the curry and serve at once.

STEP 2

STEP 3

PREPARATION

You will find this dish is even tastier if made the day before as this allows time for the flavours to blend and develop. Make the curry to the end of step 3, cool and store in the refrigerator until required. Reheat it gently until piping hot before adding the finishing touches.

STEP 4

STEP 1

STEP 2

STEP 3

STEP 4

PORK CHOPS & SPICY RED BEANS

A tasty and substantial dish that is packed full of goodness. The spicy bean mixture, served on its own, also makes a good accompaniment to meat or chicken dishes.

SERVES 4

3 tbsp ghee or vegetable oil
4 pork chops, rind removed
2 onions, thinly sliced
2 garlic cloves, crushed
2 fresh green chillies, deseeded and chopped
  or use 1–2 tsp minced chilli (from a jar)
2.5 cm / 1 inch piece ginger root, chopped
1½ tsp cumin seeds
1½ tsp ground coriander
600 ml / 1 pint / 2½ cups stock or water
2 tbsp tomato purée (paste)
½ aubergine (eggplant), trimmed and cut
  into 1 cm / ½ inch dice
salt
439 g / 14 oz can red kidney beans, drained
4 tbsp double (heavy) cream

1 Heat the ghee or oil in a large frying pan (skillet), add the pork chops and fry until sealed and browned on both sides. Remove from the pan and reserve.

2 Add the sliced onions, garlic, chillies, ginger and spices and fry gently for 2 minutes. Stir in the stock, tomato purée (paste), aubergine (eggplant) and salt to taste.

3 Bring the mixture to the boil, place the chops on top, then cover and simmer gently over a medium heat for 30 minutes, or until the chops are tender and cooked through.

4 Remove the chops and stir the red kidney beans and cream into the mixture. Return the chops to the pan, cover and heat through gently for 5 minutes. Taste and adjust the seasoning, if necessary. Serve hot.

VARIATIONS

Use lamb chops instead of pork chops, if wished. Canned chick-peas (garbanzo beans) and black-eyed beans (peas) are also delicious cooked this way in place of the red kidney beans (remember to drain and rinse them first before adding them to the pan).

STEP 1

STEP 2

STEP 2

STEP 3

LAMB & POTATO MASALA

It's so easy to create delicious Indian dishes at home – simply add a few interesting ingredients to a basic sauce and you have a splendid dish that is sure to be popular with family or friends.

SERVES 4

750 g/1½ lb lean lamb (from the leg)
4 tbsp ghee or vegetable oil
500 g/1 lb potatoes, cut into 2.5 cm/
* 1 inch pieces*
1 large onion, quartered and sliced
2 garlic cloves, crushed
175 g/6 oz mushrooms, thickly sliced
283 g/10 oz can tikka masala sauce
300 ml/½ pint/1¼ cups water
3 tomatoes, halved and cut into thin slices
125g/4 oz spinach
salt
sprigs of fresh mint to garnish

1 Cut the lamb into 2.5 cm/1 inch cubes. Heat the ghee or oil in a large pan, add the lamb and fry over moderate heat for 3 minutes or until sealed all over. Remove from the pan.

2 Add the potatoes, onion, garlic and mushrooms and fry for 3–4 minutes, stirring frequently. Stir the curry sauce and water into the pan, add the lamb, mix well and season with salt to taste. Cover and cook very gently for 1 hour or until the lamb is tender and cooked through, stirring occasionally.

3 Add the sliced tomatoes and the spinach to the pan, pushing the leaves well down into the mixture, then cover and cook for a further 10 minutes until the spinach is cooked and tender. Garnish with mint sprigs and serve hot.

SPINACH LEAVES

Spinach leaves wilt quickly during cooking, so if the leaves are young and tender add them whole to the mixture; larger leaves may be coarsely shredded, if wished, before adding to the pan.

CHAPTER TWELVE

Accompaniments

✿

No Indian-style meal is complete without a bowl of fluffy basmati rice, a mixed vegetable side dish (often curried), spicy lentils or at the very least a small bowl of natural yogurt with some diced fruit and vegetables such as cucumber, carrot, banana, tomato and onion, often flavoured with mint or coriander (cilantro).

Delicately scented basmati rice, enhanced with the flavour of mild spices, makes the standard accompaniment, but to ring the changes consider coconut rice with its richer and more distinctive coconut flavouring. Mixed vegetable bhajis lend extra variety to a meal as do potatoes cooked with typically Indian spices.

These extras all combine to give an Indian meal extra flavour and texture. Supplement them with a wide range of ready-made breads like poppadoms, naan bread (plain or spiced) and stuffed samosas, not forgetting fruity relishes like mango, and pickles with a kick, like lime.

Opposite: *Chilli peppers drying in the sun. Chillies are frequently used in Indian cooking, but be careful to remove the seeds unless you like your food very hot indeed.*

AROMATIC PILAU

This rice dish forms the perfect accompaniment to most main courses. It can be prepared ahead of time and reheated in the microwave oven just before serving.

STEP 1

STEP 2

STEP 3

STEP 4

SERVES 4–5

250 g/8 oz/1¼ cups basmati rice
2 tbsp ghee or vegetable oil
1 onion, chopped
3 cardamom pods, crushed
3 black peppercorns
3 cloves
1 tsp cumin seeds
½ cinnamon stick or piece of cassia bark
½ tsp ground turmeric
600 ml/1 pint/2½ cups boiling water or
   stock
60 g/2 oz/⅓ cup seedless raisins or sultanas
60 g/2 oz frozen peas
30 g/1 oz/¼ cup toasted, flaked (slivered)
   almonds
salt and pepper
crisp fried onion rings to garnish (optional)

 Place the rice in a sieve (strainer) and wash well under cold running water until the water runs clear. Drain.

2 Heat the oil in a large frying pan (skillet), add the onion and spices and fry gently for 1 minute, stirring all the time. Stir in the rice and mix well until coated in the spiced oil, then add the boiling water or stock and season with salt and pepper to taste.

3 Bring to the boil, stir well, then cover, reduce the heat and cook gently for 15 minutes without uncovering. Add the raisins and peas, re-cover and leave to stand for 15 minutes.

4 Uncover, fluff up with a fork and stir the toasted flaked almonds into the mixture. Serve hot, garnished with crisp fried onion rings, if liked.

S P I C E S

The whole spices used for flavouring the rice are not meant to be eaten and may be removed from the mixture, if wished, before serving.

STEP 1

STEP 2

STEP 2

STEP 3

DAL WITH SPINACH

Continental lentils are cooked in a delicious blend of spinach, onion, garlic and spices. Okra, also known as bhindi or ladies' fingers, are a favourite vegetable in Indian cooking.

SERVES 4

250 g/ 8 oz/ 1 cup continental lentils
1.25 litres/ 2¼ pints/ 5 cups water
6 tbsp vegetable oil
1 large onion, chopped
1 leek, shredded
350 g/ 12 oz spinach, shredded coarsely
1 red (bell) pepper, chopped
2–3 garlic cloves, peeled and crushed
1–2 tsp minced chilli (from a jar)
1½–2 tsp cumin seeds
1½–2 tsp ground coriander
salt and pepper
mango chutney to serve

1 Place the lentils in a sieve (strainer) and rinse well under cold running water. Drain, then place in a saucepan with the water. Bring to the boil, cover and cook for 30 minutes until the lentils are tender and the liquid has been absorbed.

2 Meanwhile, heat the oil in a large saucepan and add the chopped onion, leek, shredded spinach and red (bell) pepper. Fry gently for 8 minutes, stirring and turning frequently until the spinach has wilted. Stir in the garlic, chilli and spices and fry gently for a further 2 minutes.

3 When the lentils are cooked, uncover and shake the pan over a moderate heat for a few moments to dry off. Add the lentils to the saucepan containing the spinach and onion mixture and toss together. Season with salt and pepper to taste and serve hot, with mango chutney.

SPINACH

Fresh spinach is used in this recipe, although frozen leaf spinach (not chopped) may be used instead if more convenient. You will require 250g/8 oz frozen spinach, and it should be thawed and squeezed dry before using.

STEP 2

STEP 2

STEP 3

STEP 4

COCONUT RICE

A delicious rice dish flavoured with coconut and lemon. For a luxurious touch you can garnish each serving with a few shelled, chopped pistachio nuts.

SERVES 4–5

250 g/ 8 oz/ 1¼ cups basmati rice
3 tbsp ghee or vegetable oil
1 onion, chopped
2 garlic cloves, crushed
2.5 cm/ 1 inch piece ginger root, chopped
½ cinnamon stick or piece of cassia bark
2 carrots, grated
600 ml/ 1 pint/ 2½ cups boiling water or
    stock
30 g/ 1 oz creamed coconut, chopped finely
finely grated rind of ½ lemon or 1 lime
1 tbsp chopped fresh coriander (cilantro)
1 bunch spring onions (scallions), sliced
salt and pepper

1 Place the rice in a sieve (strainer) and wash well under cold running water until the water runs clear. Drain well.

2 Heat the ghee or oil in a large saucepan, add the onion, garlic, ginger and cinnamon and fry gently for 1 minute. Stir in the rice and carrots and mix until well coated with the oil.

3 Stir in the water or stock and season with salt and pepper. Bring to the boil, cover, reduce the heat and simmer gently for 15 minutes without taking off the lid.

4 Add the creamed coconut, lemon rind, chopped coriander (cilantro) and spring onions (scallions), fork through and serve immediately.

FOR A SPICIER VERSION

A little garam masala, sprinkled over the rice just before serving adds an interesting 'warm' spiciness to this rice dish. If a more fiery flavour is required, fork a little slivered fresh chilli (or minced chilli from a jar) through the rice at step 4.

MIXED VEGETABLE BHAJI

In this delicious dish, the vegetables are first par-boiled and then lightly braised with onions, tomatoes and spices.

STEP 1

SERVES 4–6

1 small cauliflower
125 g/4 oz French (green) beans
2 potatoes
4 tbsp ghee or vegetable oil
1 onion, chopped
2 garlic cloves, crushed
5 cm/2 inch piece ginger root, cut into fine
    slivers
1 tsp cumin seeds
2 tbsp medium curry paste
425 g/14 oz can chopped tomatoes
150 ml/¼ pint/⅔ cup water
chopped fresh coriander (cilantro) to garnish

1 Break the cauliflower into florets. Top, tail and halve the beans. Peel and quarter the potatoes lengthways, then cut each quarter into 3 pieces. Cook all the vegetables in a pan of boiling, salted water for 8 minutes. Drain well, return to the pan and shake dry over a low heat for a few moments.

2 Heat the ghee or oil in a large frying pan (skillet), add the onion, garlic, ginger and cumin seeds and stir-fry gently for 3 minutes. Stir in the curry paste, tomatoes and water and bring to the boil. Reduce the heat and simmer the spicy mixture for 2 minutes.

3 Stir in the par-cooked vegetables and mix lightly. Cover and cook gently for 5–8 minutes until just tender and cooked through. Sprinkle with the chopped coriander (cilantro). Serve hot.

STEP 1

POTATO ALTERNATIVES

New potatoes are ideal for this dish as they have a more waxy texture and retain their shape better than old (main crop) potatoes which, when overcooked, become floury and lose their shape. You could use turnip or pumpkin instead of potatoes, if preferred.

STEP 2

STEP 3

APPETIZERS

•

VEGETABLES & PULSES

•

RICE & BREADS

•

CHUTNEYS & RELISHES

•

DESSERTS & DRINKS

4

SIDE DISHES
& DESSERTS

CHAPTER THIRTEEN

Appetizers

❀

As in the rest of Asia, all the dishes in an Indian meal are usually served at once, rather than in separate courses. However, as some people may prefer to eat Indian food in a Western style, and begin with an appetizer of some kind, here is a selection of tasty morsels. The Spicy Bites in this section are exactly the kind of thing that one might nibble with drinks on a social visit or while the main course of an Indian meal is being prepared.

Many of these dishes would also be ideal for taking on a picnic, a favourite Indian family pastime. A common Sunday activity is to take a picnic to the town *maidan* or green space and spend a long lazy afternoon with family and friends chatting, eating and snoozing, and maybe throwing a few cricket balls at a makeshift wicket!

Opposite: *The unmistakable profile of the Taj Mahal.*

STEP 1

STEP 3

STEP 3

STEP 4

BITE-SIZED BHAJIS

Don't be surprised at the shape these form – they are odd but look lovely when arranged on a tray with the yogurt dipping sauce. They make an ideal snack to serve with pre-dinner drinks.

MAKES 20

2 heaped tbsp gram flour (chick-pea
  (garbanzo bean) flour)
$\frac{1}{2}$ tsp turmeric
$\frac{1}{2}$ tsp cumin seeds, ground
1 tsp garam masala
pinch of cayenne
1 egg
1 large onion, quartered and sliced
1 tbsp chopped fresh coriander (cilantro)
3 tbsp breadcrumbs (optional)
oil for deep-frying
salt
coriander (cilantro) leaves to garnish

SAUCE:
1 tsp coriander seeds, ground
$1\frac{1}{2}$ tsp cumin seeds, ground
250 ml/ 8 fl oz/ 1 cup natural yogurt
salt and pepper

1 Put the gram flour into a large bowl and mix in the spices. Make a well in the centre and add the egg. Stir to form a gluey mixture. Add the onion and sprinkle on a little salt. Add the coriander (cilantro) and stir. If the mixture is not stiff enough, add the breadcrumbs.

2 Heat the oil for deep-frying over a medium heat until fairly hot – it should just be starting to smoke.

3 Push a teaspoonful of the mixture into the oil with a second teaspoon to form fairly round balls. The bhajis should firm up quite quickly. Cook in batches of 8–10. Keep stirring them so that they brown evenly. Drain on plenty of paper towels and keep them warm in the oven until ready to serve.

4 To make the sauce, roast the spices in a frying pan (skillet). Remove from the heat and stir in the yogurt. Season well. Garnish with coriander (cilantro) leaves and serve with the bhajis.

USING HOT OIL

Make sure that the pan and all the utensils are properly dried before use. Do not let any water come into contact with the hot oil or the oil will spit and splutter, which could be dangerous.

STEP 2

STEP 3

STEP 4

STEP 5

TUNA PARCELS

I first encountered this recipe in a Fijian-Indian restaurant in Sydney. In order to quell our hunger as we waited for our food, we were served with these memorable tuna parcels. Each filling recipe makes enough to fill all the pastry.

MAKES 32

PASTRY:
500 g/1 lb/4 cups plain (all-purpose) flour
1/2 tsp turmeric
1/2 tsp salt
100 g/3 1/2 oz/scant 1/2 cup ghee
about 200 ml/7 fl oz/scant 1 cup milk, mixed with a little lemon juice

TUNA FILLING:
1/2 tsp each of turmeric and cayenne
1 tsp ground cumin
1 tsp ground coriander
200 g/7 oz can of tuna, drained
60 g/2 oz/1/3 cup frozen peas, cooked
60 g/2 oz/1/2 cup boiled potatoes, diced
salt and pepper

VEGETARIAN FILLING:
250 g/8oz white potatoes, boiled
1/2 × 425 g/14 oz can artichoke hearts, drained and puréed
1 tsp black pepper, ground
2 tsp coriander seeds, ground
1 tsp cumin seeds, ground
1/2 tsp fenugreek seeds, ground
2 large tomatoes, peeled and deseeded
90g/3 oz/1/2 cup frozen peas, cooked

SAUCE:
6 anchovies
2 tbsp natural yogurt

1 To make the pastry, sift the flour, turmeric and salt into a bowl. Rub in the ghee. Add enough milk to form a fairly soft dough. Cover and set aside.

2 To make the tuna filling, roast the spices in a large frying pan (skillet). Remove from the heat and add the tuna, peas and potatoes. Stir well and season. Continue from step 4.

3 To make the vegetarian filling, mash the potatoes and combine with the artichokes. Roast the spices in a large frying pan (skillet). Remove from the heat and add the potato mixture. Stir well to combine. Chop the tomatoes and carefully fold in with the peas. Season.

4 Roll out the pastry and cut out 16 12 cm/5 inch circles. Cut each circle in half and put a teaspoonful of filling on each half.

5 Brush the edges with milk and fold each half over to form a triangle. Seal well, and crimp the edges. Bake in a preheated oven at 190°C/375°F/Gas Mark 5.

6 To make the sauce, mash the anchovies, mix with the yogurt and season. Serve with the hot parcels.

STEP 1: Nuts

STEP 2: Nuts

STEP 2: Mussels

STEP 3: Mussels

SPICY BITES

Here are three ideas designed to whet the appetite before the meal or to eat between courses with drinks. For the Deep-Fried Vegetables, use courgettes (zucchini) with the flowers attached, if you can find them.

SERVES 4

SPICED NUTS:
125 g/4 oz/1 cup mixed nuts, such as
*   peanuts, cashews and blanched almonds*
1 dried red chilli
1 tsp sunflower oil
1 garlic clove
¹/₂ tsp salt
1 tsp garam masala
¹/₂ tsp clear honey

1 Cook the nuts in a dry, heavy-based pan over a moderate heat until the oil comes off, about 5 minutes.

2 Add the remaining ingredients except the honey, and cook for a further 3 minutes, stirring frequently. Add the honey and cook for 2 minutes.

3 Remove from the heat, turn into a serving dish and serve.

MUSSEL MORSELS:
1 kg/2 lb small mussels, scrubbed
3 tbsp mayonnaise
1 tsp garam masala
¹/₂ red chilli, deseeded and chopped finely
2 spring onions (scallions), chopped finely
45 g/1¹/₂ oz/³/₄ cup white breadcrumbs
salt

1 Put a little water in a large pan. Discard any mussels that are not closed. Add the mussels, cover and cook over a high heat for 5 minutes.

2 Drain the mussels and discard any unopened ones. Remove the shells and reserve.

3 Chop the mussels finely and mix with the mayonnaise. Add the remaining ingredients and season to taste. Spoon the mixture back into the shells, and arrange on a plate.

DEEP-FRIED VEGETABLES:
125 g/4 oz/1 cup plain (all-purpose) flour
¹/₂ tsp each turmeric and chilli powder
150 ml/¹/₄ pint/²/₃ cup water
2 eggs
vegetable oil
mixed vegetables, eg, courgettes (zucchini),
*   aubergines (eggplants)*

1 Sift the flour and spices together, Add the water, eggs and 1 tablespoon oil. Whisk until smooth.

2 Heat some oil in a wok. Dip the vegetables into the batter, and drop into the oil. When evenly cooked, remove and drain on paper towels.

STEP 1

STEP 2

STEP 3

STEP 4

BUTTERFLY PRAWNS (SHRIMP)

*These prawns (shrimp) look stunning when presented on the skewers,
and they will certainly be an impressive prelude to the main meal.*

SERVES 2–4

8 wooden skewers
500 g/ 1 lb or 16 raw tiger prawns
    (shrimp), shelled, leaving tails intact
juice of 2 limes
1 tsp cardamom seeds
2 tsp cumin seeds, ground
2 tsp coriander seeds, ground
½ tsp ground cinnamon
1 tsp ground turmeric
1 garlic clove, crushed
1 tsp cayenne
2 tbsp oil
cucumber slices to garnish

1 Soak 8 wooden skewers in water for 20 minutes. Cut the prawns (shrimp) lengthways in half down to the tail, so that they flatten out to a symmetrical shape.

2 Thread a prawn (shrimp) on to 2 wooden skewers, with the tail between them, so that, when laid flat, the skewers hold the prawn (shrimp) in shape. Thread another 3 prawns (shrimp) on to these 2 skewers in the same way. Repeat until you have 4 sets of 4 prawns (shrimp) each.

3 Lay the skewered prawns (shrimp) in a non-porous, non-metallic dish, and sprinkle over the lime juice.

4 Combine the spices and the oil, and coat the prawns (shrimp) well in the mixture.

5 Cover and chill for 4 hours.

6 Cook over a hot barbecue or in a grill (broiler) pan lined with foil under a preheated grill (broiler) for 6 minutes, turning once.

7 Serve immediately, garnished with cucumber and accompanied by a sweet chutney.

RAW PRAWNS (SHRIMP)

When marinating or stir-frying with prawns (shrimp), try to use the raw ones, as they will take up the flavours in the dish that you are cooking. They are widely available frozen, and sometimes fresh from the fishmonger.

CHAPTER FOURTEEN

Vegetables & Pulses

❀

After an Indian meal, whether it be in India or in a restaurant elsewhere or somebody's home, I'm usually left longing for a little greenery, or salad or crunchy vegetables after so many rich sauces and cooked dishes. So I have included here a few options to balance your Indian meal with some vegetable dishes.

If your main meal consists of a meat with sauce, such as Rogan Josh or Tikka Masala, try accompanying it with the Kashmiri Spinach or the deliciously simple Spicy Cauliflower. For a dry tandoori or Biryani try pairing it with the Roasted Aubergine (Eggplant) Curry for a balanced meal.

The Okra Bhaji, a dry curry dish, could be paired with a lentil dish for a simple Indian meal, as could other vegetable and dal dishes. The flavours of a bhaji are hidden in the very small amount of sauce that you are left with at the end of the cooking time, so do not be deceived into thinking that as there is no sauce, there is no flavour.

Opposite: *A fruit market is held by the side of a canal in southern India.*

STEP 3

STEP 4

STEP 5

STEP 6

OKRA BHAJI

This is a very mild-tasting, rich curry, which would be an ideal accompaniment to a tomato-based main-course curry.

SERVES 4

1 tbsp sunflower oil
1 tsp black mustard seeds
1 tsp cumin seeds
1 tsp coriander seeds, ground
$^1/_2$ tsp turmeric
1 green chilli, deseeded, chopped finely and
  rinsed
1 red onion, sliced finely
2 garlic cloves, crushed
1 orange (bell) pepper, sliced finely
500 g/ 1 lb okra, trimmed and blanched
250 ml/8 fl oz/ 1 cup vegetable juice
150 ml/$^1/_4$ pint/$^2/_3$ cup single (light) cream
1 tbsp lemon juice
salt

1 Heat the oil in a wok or large frying pan (skillet). Add the mustard seeds and cover the pan until they start to pop. Stir in the cumin seeds and ground coriander, turmeric and chilli. Stir until fragrant, about 1 minute.

2 Add the onion, garlic and (bell) pepper, and cook until soft, about 5 minutes, stirring frequently.

3 Add the okra to the pan and combine all the ingredients thoroughly.

4 Pour in the vegetable juice, bring to the boil and cook over a high heat for 5 minutes, stirring occasionally.

5 When most of the liquid has evaporated, check the seasoning.

6 Add the cream, bring to the boil again and continue to cook the mixture over a high heat for about 12 minutes until almost dry.

7 Sprinkle over the lemon juice and serve immediately.

OKRA

Okra, or lady's fingers, have a remarkable glutinous quality which, when they are added to curries and casseroles, disperses in the sauce and thickens it wonderfully – and naturally!

STEP 1

STEP 2

STEP 3

STEP 4

CURRIED ROAST POTATOES

This is the kind of Indian-inspired dish that would fit easily into any Western menu. Delicious on a buffet, or a surprise accompaniment to a traditional roast dinner – or how about serving with a curry in place of the more traditional rice?

SERVES 4

2 tsp cumin seeds
2 tsp coriander seeds
90 g/ 3 oz/^{1}/$_3$ cup salted butter
1 tsp ground turmeric
1 tsp black mustard seeds
2 garlic cloves, crushed
2 dried red chillies
750 g/ 1^1/$_2$ lb baby new potatoes
salt and pepper

1 Grind the cumin and coriander seeds together in a pestle and mortar or spice grinder. Grinding them fresh like this captures all of the flavour before it has a chance to dry out.

2 Melt the butter gently in a roasting tin (pan) and add the turmeric, mustard seeds, garlic and chillies and the ground cumin and coriander seeds. Stir well to combine evenly. Place in a preheated oven at 200°C/400°F/Gas Mark 6 for 5 minutes.

3 Remove the tin (pan) from the oven – the spices should be very fragrant at this stage – and add the potatoes. Stir well so that the butter and spice mix coats the potatoes completely.

4 Put back in the preheated oven and bake for 20–25 minutes. Stir occasionally to ensure that the potatoes are coated evenly. Test the potatoes with a skewer – if they drop off the end of the skewer when lifted, they are done. Serve immediately.

POTATOES

Baby new potatoes are now available all year round from supermarkets. However, they are not essential for this recipe. Red or white old potatoes can be substituted, cut into 2.5 cm/1 inch cubes. You can also try substituting parsnips, carrots or turnips, peeled and cut into 2.5 cm/1 inch cubes. Peel 250 g/8 oz pickling onions and mix in with the vegetables for a tasty variation.

SPICY CAULIFLOWER

This is a perfectly delicious way to serve cauliflower. It is a dry dish so can be enjoyed as a salad or at a picnic, or as an accompaniment to a dhansak or korma.

STEP 1

SERVES 4

500 g/1 lb cauliflower, cut into florets
1 tbsp sunflower oil
1 garlic clove
¹/₂ tsp turmeric
1 tsp cumin seeds, ground
1 tsp coriander seeds, ground
1 tsp yellow mustard seeds
12 spring onions (scallions), sliced finely
salt and pepper

1 Blanch the cauliflower in boiling water, drain and set aside. Cauliflower holds a lot of water, which tends to make it over-soft, so turn the florets upside-down at this stage and you will end up with a crisper result.

2 Heat the oil gently in a large, heavy frying pan (skillet) or wok. Add the garlic clove, turmeric, ground cumin, ground coriander and mustard seeds. Stir well and cover the pan.

3 When you hear the mustard seeds popping, add the spring onions (scallions) and stir. Cook for 2 minutes, stirring constantly, to soften them a little. Season to taste.

4 Add the cauliflower and stir for 3–4 minutes until coated completely with the spices and thoroughly heated.

5 Remove the garlic clove and serve immediately.

STEP 2

BABY CAULIFLOWERS

For a weekend feast or a special occasion this dish looks great made with baby cauliflowers instead of florets. Baby vegetables are more widely available nowadays, and the baby cauliflowers look very appealing on the plate. Peel off most of the outer leaves, leaving a few small ones for decoration. Blanch the baby cauliflowers whole for 4 minutes and drain. Continue as in step 2.

STEP 3

STEP 4

STEP 1

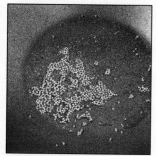

STEP 2

STEP 3

STEP 5

KASHMIRI SPINACH

*This is an imaginative way to serve spinach, which adds a little zip to it.
It is a very simple dish, which will complement almost any curry.*

SERVES 4

2 tbsp mustard oil
$^{1}/_{4}$ tsp garam masala
1 tsp yellow mustard seeds
500g/1lb spinach, washed (Swiss chard or
   baby leaf spinach may be substituted –
   baby leaf spinach needs no preparation)
sliced spring onions to garnish

1 Remove the tough stalks from the spinach.

2 Heat the mustard oil in a wok or large heavy frying pan (skillet) until it smokes. Add the garam masala and mustard seeds. Cover the pan quickly – you will hear the mustard seeds popping inside.

3 When the popping has ceased, remove the cover and stir in the spinach until wilted.

4 Continue cooking the spinach, uncovered, over a medium heat for 10–15 minutes, until most of the water has evaporated. If using frozen spinach, it will not need as much cooking – cook it only until most of the water has evaporated.

5 Remove the spinach with a perforated spoon in order to drain off any remaining liquid. This dish is more pleasant to eat when it is served as dry as possible.

6 Garnish with sliced spring onions and serve immediately while it is piping hot.

MUSTARD OIL

Mustard oil is made from mustard seeds and is very fiery when raw. However, when it is heated to this smoking stage, it loses a lot of the fire and takes on a delightful sweet quality. It is quite common in Asian cuisine, and you should find it in any Indian or oriental store.

STEP 1

STEP 2

STEP 3

STEP 4

ROASTED AUBERGINE (EGGPLANT) CURRY

This is a rich vegetable dish, ideal served with a tandoori chicken and naan bread. Also delicious as a vegetarian dish with rice.

SERVES 6

2 whole aubergines (eggplants)
250 ml/8 fl oz/1 cup natural yogurt
2 cardamom pods
½ tsp ground turmeric
1 dried red chilli
½ tsp coriander seeds
½ tsp pepper
1 tsp garam masala
1 clove
2 tbsp sunflower oil
1 onion, sliced lengthways
2 garlic cloves, crushed
1 tbsp grated ginger root
6 ripe tomatoes, peeled, deseeded and
    quartered
sprigs of fresh coriander (cilantro) to
    garnish

1 If you have a gas cooker, roast the 2 aubergines (eggplants) over a naked flame, turning frequently, until charred and black all over (for other methods see box, right). This should take about 5 minutes. Peel under running cold water. Cut off the stem and discard.

2 Put the peeled aubergines (eggplants) into a large bowl and mash lightly with a fork. Stir in the yogurt. Set aside.

3 Grind together the cardamom pods, turmeric, red chilli, coriander seeds, pepper, garam masala and clove in a large pestle and mortar or spice grinder.

4 Heat the oil in a wok or heavy frying pan (skillet) over a moderate heat and cook the onion, garlic and ginger root until soft. Add the tomatoes and ground spices, and stir well.

5 Add the aubergine (eggplant) mixture to the pan and stir well. Cook for 5 minutes over a gentle heat, stirring constantly, until all the flavours are combined, and some of the liquid has evaporated. Serve immediately, garnished with coriander (cilantro).

VARIATION

The aubergines (eggplants) can be cooked over the barbecue, in which case they will char in a shorter time, with frequent turning. Alternatively, they can be cooked in a very hot oven for 15 minutes, turning once, although this method will not give the rich, smoky flavour to the aubergine (eggplant) that makes this dish so distinctive.

STEP 1

STEP 2

STEP 3

STEP 4

LONG BEANS WITH TOMATOES

I often feel that Indian meals need some green vegetables to complement the spicy dishes and to set off the rich sauces. I have created this dish as a side order for tandooris, rogan josh or biryani. It will go with most Indian dishes.

SERVES 4–6

500 g/1 lb green beans, cut into 5 cm/
*   2 inch lengths*
2 tbsp ghee
2.5 cm/1 inch piece ginger root, grated
1 garlic clove, crushed
1 tsp turmeric
1/2 tsp cayenne
1 tsp ground coriander
4 tomatoes, peeled, deseeded and diced
150 ml/1/4 pint/2/3 cup vegetable stock

1 Blanch the beans quickly in boiling water, drain and refresh under cold running water.

2 Melt the ghee in a large saucepan. Add the grated ginger root and crushed garlic, stir and add the turmeric, cayenne and ground coriander. Stir until fragrant, about 1 minute.

3 Add the tomatoes, tossing them until they are thoroughly coated in the spice mix.

4 Add the vegetable stock to the pan, bring to the boil and cook over a medium-high heat for 10 minutes, until the sauce has thickened, stirring occasionally.

5 Add the beans, reduce the heat to moderate and heat through for 5 minutes, stirring.

6 Transfer to a serving dish and serve immediately.

GINGER GRATERS

Ginger graters are an invaluable piece of equipment to have when cooking Indian food. These small flat graters, made of either bamboo or china, can be held directly over the pan while you grate. They have an ingenious way of dealing with ginger, which leaves most of the tough stringy bits behind.

YELLOW SPLIT PEA CASSEROLE

If ever there was a winter warmer, this is it – an intensely satisfying dish, ideal for serving with a lightweight main dish such as pilau or biryani, but equally good with a richer curry and fresh naan bread.

SERVES 6

2 tbsp ghee
1 tsp black mustard seeds
1 onion, chopped finely
2 garlic cloves, crushed
1 carrot, grated
2.5 cm/1 inch piece ginger root, grated
1 green chilli, deseeded and chopped finely
1 tbsp tomato purée (paste)
250 g/8 oz/1 cup yellow split peas, soaked
    in water for 2 hours
400 g/13 oz can chopped tomatoes
500 ml/16 fl oz/2 cups vegetable stock
250 g/8 oz/1½ cups pumpkin, cubed
250 g/8 oz cauliflower, cut into florets
2 tbsp oil
1 large aubergine (eggplant), cubed
1 tbsp chopped fresh coriander (cilantro)
1 tsp garam masala
salt and pepper

STEP 2

1 Melt the ghee over a medium heat in a large pan. Add the mustard seeds, and when they start to splutter, add the onion, garlic, carrot, and ginger. Cook until soft, about 5 minutes. Add the green chilli and stir in the tomato purée (paste). Stir in the split peas.

2 Add the tomatoes and stock, and bring to the boil. Season well.

3 Simmer for 40 minutes, stirring occasionally. Add the pumpkin cubes and cauliflower florets, and simmer for a further 30 minutes, covered, until the split peas are soft.

4 Meanwhile, heat the oil in a frying pan (skillet) over a high heat. Add the aubergine (eggplant), and stir until sealed on all sides; remove and drain on paper towels.

5 Stir the aubergine (eggplant) into the split pea mixture with the coriander (cilantro) and garam masala. Check for seasoning.

6 Transfer to a serving dish and serve immediately.

STEP 3

TIPS

When cooking with pulses and legumes, be sure that you do not over-stir, as this will break up the individual peas or beans.

To transform this recipe into a one-pot meal, simply add some cooked meat such as bacon, lamb or duck.

STEP 4

STEP 2

STEP 3

STEP 4

STEP 5

COOL BEAN SALAD

This is a delicious 'Indian Summer' dish, ideal for serving at a barbecue, or to accompany one of the hotter Indian curries, or served as part of a salad buffet at parties – just remember to remove the garlic.

SERVES 4

1 red onion, finely sliced
350 g/12 oz/3 cups broad (fava) beans,
  fresh or frozen
150 ml/¼ pint/⅔ cup natural yogurt
1 tbsp chopped fresh mint
½ tbsp lemon juice
1 garlic clove, halved
salt and ground white pepper
½ cucumber, peeled, halved and sliced

1 Rinse the red onion slices briefly under cold running water, and drain well.

2 Put the broad (fava) beans into a pan of boiling water and cook until tender, 8–10 minutes for fresh, 5–6 minutes for frozen. Drain, rinse under the cold tap and drain again.

3 Shell the beans from their white outer shells, and you are left with the sweet green bean. This is optional, but well worth the effort.

4 Combine the yogurt, mint, lemon juice, garlic and seasoning in a small bowl.

5 Combine the onion, cucumber and broad (fava) beans. Toss them in the yogurt dressing. Remove the garlic halves. Spoon on to a serving plate and serve.

RAW ONION

I find that rinsing the raw onion under the tap takes the edge off the raw taste, as it washes away some of the juices. The same technique can be used on other pungent vegetables and salad, such as spring onions (scallions), bitter cucumbers and chillies.

CHAPTER FIFTEEN

Rice & Breads

❀

Rice is a staple ingredient in Indian cooking; it is served at virtually every main meal, and acts as a filling base and a foil for the richer, spicier dishes. The stunning mountain ranges that are the Himalayas provide the crystal-clear mineral water that is used to grow basmati rice. For basmati rice to be classified as such, it must be grown in the foothills of the Himalayas. However, it is such a desirable commodity in the world market that due to 'creative' sales techniques more 'basmati' rice is sold each year than is harvested! Basmati rice has more perfume than long-grain rice, is whiter and has a longer grain.

Bread is another staple ingredient, used to mop up sauces and stews, and it makes meals easier to eat with the hands. Indian bread is very easy to make, as it needs very little kneading and rising, and is usually quickly deep-fried or dry-fried. It appears in many forms – pooris, poppadoms, oven-baked naan, pan-fried chapatis and parathas – all equally delicious.

Opposite: *Fresh food and other wares are often transported by boat along the backwaters of India.*

STEP 1

STEP 2

STEP 3

STEP 5

SAFFRON RICE

This is the classic way to serve rice, paired with saffron, so that each brings out the best in the other. To get maximum flavour from the rice, soak it overnight and drain before cooking. Reduce the cooking time by 3–4 minutes to compensate.

SERVES 8

12 saffron threads, crushed lightly
2 tbsp warm water
270 ml/14 fl oz/1³/₄ cups water
250 g/8 oz basmati rice
1 tbsp toasted, flaked (slivered) almonds

1 Put the saffron threads into a bowl with the warm water and leave for 10 minutes. They need to be crushed before soaking to ensure that the maximum flavour and colour is extracted at this stage.

2 Put the water and rice into a medium saucepan and set it over the heat to boil. Add the saffron and saffron water and stir.

3 Bring back to a gentle boil, stir again and let the rice simmer, uncovered, for about 10 minutes, until all the water has been absorbed.

4 Cover tightly, reduce the heat as much as possible and leave for 10 minutes. Do not remove the lid. This ensures that the grains separate and that the rice is not soggy.

5 Remove from the heat and transfer to a serving dish. Fork through the rice gently and sprinkle on the toasted almonds before serving.

SAFFRON

Saffron is the most ancient of spices and continues to be the most expensive – literally worth its weight in gold. It is still harvested and sorted by hand and is a treasured commodity. The purest, strongest saffron – La Mancha grade – is not easily found. Saffron is grown in Europe and the Middle East and is found worldwide in food and drinks. It is used in England for Cornish saffron cake, in Italy for risotto, in France for bouillabaisse and in Spain for paella.

Saffron stigmas are wiry, 2.5 cm/1 inch long and a vibrant reddish-orange or sometimes yellow colour – the deeper colour is the better quality. Powdered saffron may be substituted for the threads. This is usually a very low grade of saffron that has been heavily adulterated. Although it will not give the flavour, it provides a pleasing colour, though the dish will lack the extra visual appeal of the threads trailing through the rice.

STEP 1

STEP 2

STEP 3

STEP 4

HYDERABAD RICE PILAU

This is a wonderfully colourful and complex pilau, full of spice and flavour and aromatic ingredients, from exotic okra to saffron and hot chilli powder. Though it is quite simple to make, it looks very impressive on the dinner table.

SERVES 6

3 tbsp sunflower oil
1 onion, sliced finely
3 shallots, chopped finely
1 garlic clove, crushed
1 tsp grated ginger root
425 g/14 oz/2 cups basmati rice
½ tsp chilli powder
250 g/8 oz/2 cups okra, trimmed
1 litre/1¾ pints/4 cups chicken stock
1 tsp saffron, crushed lightly
pared rind of ½ orange
60 g/2 oz/⅓ cup sultanas (golden raisins)
1 tbsp lemon juice

TO GARNISH:
30 g/1 oz flaked (slivered) almonds, toasted
1 tsp chopped fresh mint
1 tsp chopped fresh coriander (cilantro)

1 Heat the oil in a wok or large frying pan (skillet) until quite hot. Fry the onion until golden brown, then remove and drain on paper towels. Don't cook all at once, as the slices won't be crisp.

2 Reduce the heat under the wok. Cook the shallots in the remaining oil until soft, about 5 minutes. Add the garlic and ginger, and stir. Stir in the rice, chilli powder and okra.

3 Pour in the chicken stock, saffron and orange rind. Bring to the boil and simmer over a moderate heat for 15 minutes.

4 Add the sultanas (golden raisins) at the end of this time and stir in the lemon juice.

5 Remove the piece of orange rind if you prefer, then transfer to a serving dish and garnish with the fried onion, toasted almonds, mint and coriander (cilantro).

RICE

Rice which is labelled 'pre-cooked', 'pre-fluffed', or 'easy cook' has undergone a process that drives some of the vitamin C and minerals back into the grain from the rice husk, a process which also hardens the outside of the rice so that the grains stay separate and fluffy. So never imagine that this rice is inferior – it is in fact far better for you than natural rice!

STEP 1

STEP 2

STEP 3

STEP 4

KITCHOURI

This is the dish from which kedgeree evolved. The traditional breakfast plate of smoked haddock, egg and rice reputedly has its roots in this flavoured rice dish, which the British colonists adopted and to which they added preserved fish, to make the version that we know today.

SERVES 4

2 tbsp ghee or butter
1 red onion, chopped finely
1 garlic clove, crushed
$\frac{1}{2}$ celery stick, chopped finely
1 tsp turmeric
$\frac{1}{2}$ tsp garam masala
1 green chilli, deseeded and chopped finely
$\frac{1}{2}$ tsp cumin seeds
1 tbsp chopped fresh coriander (cilantro)
125 g/4 oz/generous $\frac{1}{2}$ cup basmati rice, rinsed under cold water until water runs clear
125 g/4 oz/$\frac{1}{2}$ cup green lentils
300 ml/$\frac{1}{2}$ pint/1$\frac{1}{4}$ cups vegetable juice
600 ml/1 pint/2$\frac{1}{2}$ cups vegetable stock
sprigs of fresh coriander (cilantro) to garnish

1 Melt the ghee in a large saucepan. Add the onion, garlic and celery, and cook until soft, about 5 minutes.

2 Add the turmeric, garam masala, green chilli, cumin seeds and coriander (cilantro). Stir until fragrant over a moderate heat, about 1 minute.

3 Add the rice and green lentils, and stir until the rice is translucent, about 1 minute.

4 Pour the vegetable juice and vegetable stock into the saucepan, and bring to the boil. Cover and simmer over a low heat for about 20 minutes, or until the lentils are cooked. They should be tender when pressed between the fingers. Stir occasionally.

5 Transfer to a warmed serving dish, garnish with coriander (cilantro) sprigs and serve piping hot.

VEGETARIAN LUNCH

This is a versatile dish, and can be served as a great-tasting and satisfying one-pot meal for a vegetarian. I have also served it as a winter lunch dish with tomatoes and yogurt.

SPINACH POORI

These little nibbles are very satisfying to make. They are the most attractive green colour to start with, and when you add them to the pan, they start to puff up immediately. Don't be slow in serving them and they will still be little puffballs when you get to the table.

STEP 2

SERVES 6

125 g/4 oz/1 cup plain (all-purpose) wholemeal (whole wheat) flour
125 g/4 oz/1 cup plain (all-purpose) flour
½ tsp salt
2 tbsp vegetable oil
125 g/4 oz/½ cup chopped spinach, fresh or frozen, blanched, puréed and all excess water squeezed out
50 ml/2 fl oz/¼ cup water
oil for deep-frying

RELISH:
2 tbsp chopped fresh mint
2 tbsp natural yogurt
½ red onion, sliced and rinsed
½ tsp chilli powder
sprigs of fresh mint to garnish

1 Sift the flours and salt into a bowl. Drizzle over the oil and rub in until the mixture resembles fine breadcrumbs.

2 Add the spinach and water, and stir in to make a stiff dough. Knead for 10 minutes until smooth.

3 Form the dough into a ball. Put into an oiled bowl and turn to coat. Cover with clingfilm (plastic wrap) and set aside for 30 minutes.

4 Meanwhile, make the relish. Combine the mint, yogurt and onion, transfer to a serving bowl and sift the chilli powder over the top.

5 Knead the dough again and divide into 12 small balls. Remove 1 ball and keep the rest covered. Roll this ball out into a 12 cm/5 inch circle.

6 Put the oil into a wok or wide frying pan (skillet) to 2.5 cm/1 inch depth. Heat it until a haze appears. It must be very hot.

7 Have ready a plate lined with paper towels. Put 1 poori on the surface of the oil – if it sinks, it should rise up immediately and sizzle; if it doesn't, the oil isn't hot enough. Keep the poori submerged in the oil, using the back of a fish slice or a perforated spoon. The poori will puff up immediately. Turn it over and cook the other side for 5–10 seconds.

8 As soon as the poori is cooked, remove and drain. Repeat with the remaining balls of dough. Serve immediately with the relish, garnished with mint sprigs.

STEP 4

STEP 5

STEP 7

PARATHAS

These triangular shaped breads are so easy to make and are the perfect addition to most Indian meals. Serve hot, spread with a little butter, if wished.

STEP 1

MAKES 6

90 g/ 3 oz/³/₄ cup plain (all-purpose) wholemeal flour
90 g/ 3 oz/³/₄ cup plain (all-purpose) white flour
a good pinch of salt
1 tbsp vegetable oil, plus extra for greasing
75 ml/ 3 fl oz/¹/₃ cup tepid water

1 Place the flours and the salt in a bowl. Drizzle 1 tablespoon of oil over the flour, add the tepid water and mix to form a soft dough, adding a little more water, if necessary. Knead on a lightly floured surface until smooth, then cover and leave for 30 minutes.

2 Knead the dough on a floured surface and divide into 6 equal pieces. Shape each one into a ball. Roll out on a floured surface to a 15 cm/6 in round and brush very lightly with oil.

3 Fold in half, and then in half again to form a triangle. Roll out to form an 18 cm/7 inch triangle (when measured from point to centre top), dusting with extra flour as necessary.

4 Brush a large frying pan (skillet) with a little oil and heat until hot,

STEP 2

then add one or two parathas and cook for about 1–1½ minutes. Brush the surfaces very lightly with oil, then turn and cook the other sides for 1½ minutes until cooked through.

5 Place the cooked parathas on a plate and cover with foil, or place between a clean tea towel to keep warm, while cooking the remainder in the same way, greasing the pan between cooking each batch.

STEP 3

ALTERNATIVE

If the parathas puff up a lot during cooking, press down lightly with a fish slice. Make parathas in advance, if wished: wrap in kitchen foil and reheat in a hot oven for about 15 minutes when required.

STEP 4

STEP 6

STEP 7

STEP 7

STEP 9

PESHWARI NAAN

A tandoor oven throws out a ferocious heat; this bread is traditionally cooked on the side wall of the oven where the heat is only slightly less than in the centre. For an authentic effect, leave your grill (broiler) on for a good long time to heat up before the first dough goes under.

SERVES 4–6

50 ml/2 fl oz/¹/₄ cup warm water
pinch of sugar
¹/₂ tsp active dried yeast
500 g/1 lb/4 cups strong bread flour
¹/₂ tsp salt
50 ml/2 fl oz/¹/₄ cup natural yogurt
2 Granny Smith apples, peeled and diced
60 g/2 oz/¹/₃ cup sultanas (golden raisins)
60 g/2 oz/¹/₂ cup flaked (slivered) almonds
1 tbsp coriander (cilantro) leaves
2 tbsp grated coconut

1 Combine the water and sugar in a bowl and sprinkle over the yeast. Leave for 5–10 minutes, until the yeast has dissolved and the mixture is foamy.

2 Put the flour and salt into a large bowl and make a well in the centre. Add the yeast mixture and yogurt to the bowl. Draw the flour into the liquid, until all the flour is absorbed. Mix together, adding enough tepid water to form a soft dough, about 150 ml/¹/₄ pint/²/₃ cup.

3 Turn out on to a floured board and knead for 10 minutes until smooth and elastic. Put into an oiled bowl, cover with a cloth and leave for 3 hours in a warm place, or in the fridge overnight.

4 Line the grill (broiler) pan with foil, shiny side up.

5 Put the apples into a saucepan with a little water. Bring to the boil, mash them down, reduce the heat and continue to simmer for 20 minutes, mashing occasionally.

6 Divide the dough into 4 pieces and roll each piece out to a 20 cm/8 inch oval.

7 Pull one end to form a teardrop shape, about 5 mm/¹/₄ inch thick. Lay on a floured surface and prick all over with a fork.

8 Brush both sides of the bread with oil. Place under a preheated grill (broiler) at the highest setting. Cook for 3 minutes, turn the bread over and cook for a further 3 minutes. It should have dark brown spots all over.

9 Spread a teaspoonful of the apple purée all over the bread, then sprinkle over a quarter of the sultanas (golden raisins), the flaked (slivered) almonds, the coriander (cilantro) leaves and the coconut. Repeat with the remaining 3 ovals of dough.

CHAPTER SIXTEEN

Chutneys & Relishes

❧

In the Indian subcontinent the heat is often so intense and enveloping that it is essential for every cook to have in his or her repertoire pickle and chutney recipes which preserve a wide range of ingredients regardless of the heat. Salt, oil, vinegar and citric acid can all be used as a means of preserving, depending on the effect that you want.

These preserves have claimed their place in the grand scheme of Indian gastronomy – no table would be complete without a selection of pickles presented on a tray for you to dip into. Who could imagine eating a dry, spicy tandoori dish without a yogurt accompaniment? Or crisp poppadoms without the mango chutney? Not only do Indian pickles and preserves accompany meat and fish, but because vegetarianism is such a way of life in India, they are devised to complement the meat-free meals too.

I have tried here to demonstrate a cross-section of methods and ingredients used. Lassi yogurt drink is a delicious way of cooling down a spicy curry, or quenching your thirst on a hot summer's day – it is an essentially Indian and aromatic drink.

Opposite: *Ingredients and cooking utensils being transported by boat on a lake in Kashmir.*

STEP 1: Tomato

STEP 2: Tomato

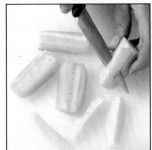

STEP 3: Tomato

STEP 4: Tomato

TOMATO, ONION & CUCUMBER KACHUMBER

This is a relish that is served at all Indian tables as a palate refresher, or an appetizer, or simply as a relish to garnish the main meal. I have included two variations on the main recipe.

EACH SERVES 6

TOMATO, ONION & CUCUMBER KACHUMBER:
3 ripe tomatoes, peeled
¼ cucumber, peeled
1 small onion, quartered
1 tsp lime juice
2 green chillies, deseeded and chopped
(optional)

1 Cut the tomatoes into quarters and cut each quarter in half. The seeds can be removed at this stage, if you prefer.

2 Cut the cucumber lengthways into quarters.

3 Remove the seeds from the cucumber, and cut into cubes.

4 Cut each onion quarter into slices.

5 Combine all the ingredients in a bowl and sprinkle with the lime juice.

6 Add the chillies, if using, and serve.

MANGO KACHUMBER:
½ mango, peeled and chopped
1 small onion, chopped
1 tbsp chopped fresh coriander (cilantro)
2 tomatoes, chopped

1 Combine all the ingredients in a bowl, and serve.

RADISH KACHUMBER:
8 large radishes, sliced
½ cucumber, peeled and chopped
1 small onion, chopped
1 tbsp chopped fresh coriander (cilantro)
1 tbsp oil
1 tbsp vinegar

1 Combine all the ingredients in a bowl, and serve.

PEELING TOMATOES

To peel tomatoes, make a little cross in the bottom of each one with a pointed knife, place in a bowl and cover with boiling water. Leave for 1 minute before draining. The skins will slip off easily.

STEP 1

STEP 2

STEP 3

STEP 4

LIME PICKLE

This is the hottest and most thirst-making of the Indian pickles. Ginger pickle is the sweetest, but lime pickle is the one that will have you going back for more!

MAKES ENOUGH FOR 2 x 500 G/1 LB JARS

6 limes, rinsed
60 g/2 oz/¹⁄₂ cup salt
1 tbsp yellow mustard seeds
1 tsp fenugreek seeds
seeds from 2 star anise
4 small green chillies, chopped finely
125 g/4 oz/²⁄₃ cup light muscovado sugar
1 tbsp ground ginger
3–4 tbsp water

1 Cut the limes into quarters, put them into a wide bowl and sprinkle over the salt. Leave for 24 hours.

2 Next day, put the mustard seeds, fenugreek, star anise seeds and chillies into a dry saucepan and cover. Place over a high heat and roast the spices, shaking the pan constantly until the mustard seeds start to pop. Remove from the heat.

3 Strain the liquid from the limes into a small pan. Add the sugar, ginger and water. Boil for 2 minutes or until the sugar has dissolved.

4 Combine the limes and toasted spices thoroughly and put into 2

clean, dry preserving jars. Pour over the sugar mixture, making sure that it covers the limes. If it doesn't, push the limes further down into the jar, or remove one or two quarters.

5 Cover the jars loosely, and when quite cool, screw on the lids tightly. Label each jar, adding the date on which the pickle was made. Keep for 4 weeks before using.

FENUGREEK

Fenugreek can be bought quite easily in supermarkets and Indian stores. It adds rather a bitter taste to recipes, which is sometimes needed – here I have used it to offset the sweetness of the sugar.

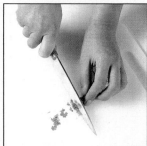

STEP 1: Cucumber

STEP 2: Cucumber

STEP 2: Cucumber

STEP 3: Cucumber

CUCUMBER RAITA

*In any Indian restaurant, the first thing to be brought to the table
should be a kachumber salad (see page 198) and a raita, which you eat
with a few poppadoms while you make a selection from the menu. Here I
have suggested three variations in addition to the original recipe.*

SERVES 4

CUCUMBER RAITA:
2 tsp fresh mint leaves
½ cucumber
250 ml/8 fl oz/1 cup natural yogurt
salt and pepper
grated nutmeg to serve

1 Chop the fresh mint finely.

2 Peel the cucumber, deseed it and
cut into matchsticks.

3 Combine the yogurt, mint and
cucumber. Season to taste.

4 Turn into a serving dish and
sprinkle over nutmeg to serve.

GRAPEFRUIT RAITA:
1 tsp sugar
1 tsp finely grated grapefruit rind
½ grapefruit, segmented
250 ml/8 fl oz/1 cup natural yogurt
salt and pepper

1 Combine all the ingredients and
serve immediately. This version
should be eaten on the day you make it,
as it does not keep for more than a day.

MELON RAITA:
*¼ honeydew or firm melon, peeled and cut
into 1 cm/½ inch cubes*
*¼ medium pineapple, peeled and cut into
1 cm/½ inch cubes*
1 tsp cayenne
1 tsp ground coriander seeds
250 ml/8 fl oz/1 cup natural yogurt
salt and pepper

1 Combine the melon and pineapple
cubes, cayenne, ground coriander
seeds and salt and pepper in a bowl. Stir
in the yogurt and serve. This will keep for
1–2 days in the refrigerator.

DATE RAITA:
6 dates, chopped
1 tbsp raisins
1 Granny Smith apple, chopped
250 ml/8 fl oz/1 cup natural yogurt
salt and pepper

1 Combine all these ingredients in a
bowl and serve. This will keep for
1–2 days in the refrigerator.

STEP 1

STEP 2

STEP 3

STEP 4

CHILLI CHUTNEY

Surprisingly enough an Indian meal isn't always hot enough for everybody. This chutney will give a bite to the meal, as well as a zingy lime freshener to the palate.

SERVES 6

1 lime, rinsed and halved, sliced very
   thinly
1 tbsp salt
2 red chillies, chopped finely
2 green chillies, chopped finely
1 tbsp white wine vinegar
1 tbsp lemon juice
$^{1}/_{2}$ tsp sugar
2 shallots, chopped finely and rinsed
1 tbsp oil

1 Combine the lime slices and salt. Leave for 30 minutes.

2 Rinse the chillies in the vinegar briefly. Drain.

3 Combine the chillies, lemon juice, sugar, shallots and oil.

4 Stir the salted limes into the other ingredients.

5 Transfer to a non-staining serving dish. Serve with any mild or richly flavoured curry.

CHILLIES

The outward appearance of a chilli is no guide to the heat content: large chillies can be blisteringly hot, and small ones can be sweet and mild, though the reverse is usually true. There are a number of ways to reduce the heat in chillies.

The chilli seeds are the hottest part of the chilli, so the simplest and most common method is to leave out the seeds altogether. Chillies give up more of their heat when they are chopped, so if you use them whole in the dish and remove them before serving, they will impart less heat to the dish. However, if you do want to slice or chop them, they can be rinsed in cold water before use, which removes a little heat. Rinsing in vinegar removes more. Also, if you blanch chopped chillies in boiling water, you discard the heat with the water.

Above all, use caution – once chillies have been added to a dish, it is more tricky to reduce the heat, although some dishes can be 'cooled' by simmering them for a while. If you do overdo it, cool your mouth by eating rice or bread, which is better than drinking lots of water.

CHAPTER SEVENTEEN

Desserts & Drinks

❀

The Indians frequently finish a meal with fresh fruit from the colourful supply available that includes mangoes, papayas, bananas, guavas and pears. Richer concoctions such as carrot halva, mango ice cream, ice cool sherbets and saffron-scented rice pudding are served only on special occasions such as a religious festival. In India they would be served on the very finest tableware and decorated with *vark*, the edible silver or gold leaf.

Saffron Spiced Rice Pudding is a true classic, but is cooked in a saucepan over a low heat rather than baked in the oven. It is very sweet, often saffron or rose-water scented and sprinkled with chopped nuts such as pistachios. It is perhaps one of the most popular of all desserts made in Indian households. Other favourites make great use of milk, yogurt and cream, including Indian Ice Cream (Kulfi) and Coconut Cream Moulds.

Do try some of these dishes, for it is true to say that Indian restaurants offer little in the way of special Indian desserts and they are always a pleasant and enjoyable experience.

Opposite: *Pavilions on Lake Gadsi-Sar, Rajasthan.*

STEP 1

STEP 2

STEP 3

STEP 3

MANGO & YOGURT CREAM

*This wonderfully refreshing dessert is designed to help refresh
the palate after a hot and spicy meal.*

SERVES 6

2 large ripe mangoes
2 tbsp lime juice
2 tbsp caster sugar
150 ml/¹/₄ pint/²/₃ cup double (heavy)
   cream
150 ml/¹/₄ pint/²/₃ cup strained thick
   yogurt
4 cardamom pods, crushed, and seeds
   removed and crushed
lime zest or twists, to decorate

1 To prepare each mango, cut along either side of the large central stone, to give two halves. Cut the remaining flesh from the stone. Scoop out the flesh and discard the skin.

2 Place the flesh in a blender or food processor with the lime juice and sugar and process until the mixture forms a smooth purée. Turn the mixture into a bowl.

3 Whip the cream in a bowl until stiff, then fold in the yogurt and the crushed cardamom seeds. Reserve 4 tablespoons of the mango purée for decoration, and mix the remaining mango purée into the cream and yogurt mixture.

4 Spoon the mixture into pretty serving glasses or dishes. Drizzle a little of the reserved mango sauce over each dessert and serve chilled, decorated with lime zest.

MANGOES

When choosing mangoes, select ones that are shiny with unblemished skins. To test if they are ripe for eating, gently cup the mango in your hand and squeeze it gently – it should give slightly to the touch if ready for eating.

STEP 1

STEP 1

STEP 2

STEP 2

AROMATIC FRUIT SALAD

*The fruits in this salad are arranged attractively on serving plates
with the spicy syrup spooned over.*

SERVES 6

*¹/₂ honeydew melon
a good-sized wedge of watermelon
2 ripe guavas
3 ripe nectarines
about 18 strawberries
a little toasted, shredded coconut for
   sprinkling
sprigs of mint or rose petals to decorate
strained thick yogurt to serve*

*SYRUP:
60 g/1¹/₂ oz/3 tbsp granulated sugar
150 ml/¹/₄ pint/²/₃ cup water
1 cinnamon stick or large piece of cassia bark
4 cardamom pods, crushed
1 clove
juice of 1 orange
juice of 1 lime*

1 To make the syrup, put the sugar,
water, cinnamon, cardamom pods
and clove into a pan and bring to the
boil, stirring to dissolve the sugar.
Simmer for 2 minutes, then remove from
heat, add the orange and lime juices and
leave to cool and infuse while preparing
the fruits.

2 Peel and remove the seeds from the
melons and cut the flesh into neat
slices. Cut the guavas in half, scoop out
the seeds, then peel and slice the flesh
neatly. Cut the nectarines into slices and
hull and slice the strawberries.

3 Arrange the slices of fruit
attractively on 6 serving plates.
Strain the prepared cooled syrup and
spoon over the sliced fruits. Sprinkle with
a little toasted coconut. Decorate with
sprigs of mint or rose petals and serve
with yogurt.

VARIATIONS

Use any exotic fruits of your choice, or
those that are in season. You can, of
course, cut up the fruits and serve them in
a bowl, in the usual way, if you prefer.

BANANAS WITH SPICED YOGURT

This simple but delicious dessert is at its best when made with thick and creamy strained yogurt.

STEP 1

SERVES 4–6

3 good pinches saffron strands
2 tbsp creamy milk
6 cardamom pods, crushed and seeds
   removed and crushed
45 g/ 1½ oz/ 3 tbsp butter
45 g/ 1½ oz/ 3 tbsp soft brown sugar
½ tsp ground cinnamon
2 bananas
500 g/ 1 lb strained thick yogurt
2-3 tbsp clear honey, to taste
30 g/ 1 oz/¼ cup toasted, flaked (slivered)
   almonds

1 Place the saffron strands on a small piece of foil and toast very lightly. Crush the saffron strands finely and place in a small bowl. Add the milk and crushed cardamom seeds, stir well and leave to cool.

2 Meanwhile, melt the butter in a frying pan, add the brown sugar and cinnamon and stir well. Peel and slice the bananas and fry gently for about 1 minute, turning halfway through cooking. Remove from the pan and place the fried banana slices in decorative serving glasses.

3 Mix the yogurt with the cold spiced milk and the honey. Spoon the mixture on top of the bananas and sprinkle the surface of each serving with toasted, flaked almonds. Chill before serving, if preferred.

STEP 2

ALTERNATIVE

The flavour of saffron strands is improved by lightly toasting before use, but do take care not to overcook them or the flavour is spoilt and becomes bitter. This delicious dessert may also be made using half cream and half yogurt and the tops could be sprinkled with unsalted, chopped pistachios instead of almonds, if wished.

STEP 2

STEP 3

STEP 2

STEP 3

STEP 4

STEP 4

COCONUT ICE CREAM

This delicious ice-cream will make the perfect ending to any Indian meal. For a smooth-textured, leave out the desiccated (shredded) coconut.

SERVES 6

150 g/5 oz/²⁄₃ cup granulated sugar
300 ml/¹⁄₂ pint/1¹⁄₄ cups water
2 x 400 ml/14 fl oz cans coconut milk
300 ml/¹⁄₂ pint/1¹⁄₄ cups double (heavy) cream
2 tbsp desiccated (shredded) coconut
rose petals or sprigs of fresh mint to decorate

1 Place the sugar and water in a saucepan and heat gently, stirring occasionally until the sugar dissolves. Boil gently for 10 minutes without stirring, then remove from the heat and allow to cool slightly.

2 Mix the cooled syrup with the coconut milk and pour into a shallow freezer container. Cover and freeze for about 3 hours or until semi-frozen around the edges and mushy in the centre.

3 Transfer the mixture to a bowl and cut up with a knife, then place (half the quantity at a time) in a food processor and process until smooth.

4 Turn the mixture into a bowl. Whip the cream until softly peaking and fold into the ice cream, then stir in the desiccated (shredded) coconut. Return the mixture to the container and freeze again until solid.

5 Before serving, remove the container of ice cream to the refrigerator and leave in the main compartment for 30 minutes (or at room temperature for 15 minutes) to soften. Scoop or spoon the ice cream into serving dishes and decorate with rose petals or sprigs of mint.

SERVING ICE-CREAM

For easy serving, scoop the ice cream into portions the night before required and place on a chilled baking tray, then freeze until ready to serve.

INDIAN ICE CREAM (KULFI)

*To make traditional kulfi is quite a time-consuming process,
so why not try this deliciously easy version instead?*

STEP 1

SERVES 6–8

75 ml/ 3 fl oz/ 5 tbsp boiling water
*4 cardamom pods, crushed and seeds
  removed*
405 g/ 14 oz can sweetened condensed milk
75 ml/ 3 fl oz/ 5 tbsp cold water
30 g/ 1 oz/ ¼ cup unsalted pistachio nuts
30 g/ 1 oz/ ¼ cup blanched almonds
2 drops almond essence (optional)
*150 ml/ ¼ pint/ ⅔ cup double (heavy)
  cream*
lime zest to decorate

1 Pour the boiling water into a bowl,
stir in the cardamom seeds and
leave for 15 minutes to infuse.
Meanwhile, put the condensed milk into
a blender or food processor together with
the cold water, pistachio nuts, almonds
and almond essence, if using. Process the
mixture for about 30 seconds until very
finely mixed. Alternatively, very finely
chop the pistachio nuts and almonds and
mix with the water and almond essence,
if using.

2 Add the cooled and strained
cardamom water and pour into a
bowl. Whip the cream until softly
peaking and whisk into the mixture.
Pour the mixture into a shallow metal or
plastic container and freeze for about 3
hours or until semi-frozen around the
edges and mushy in the centre.

STEP 2

3 Transfer the mixture to a bowl and
mash well with a fork (to break up
the ice crystals). Divide the mixture
evenly between 6–8 small moulds (see
below) and freeze for at least 4 hours or
overnight until firm.

4 To serve, dip the base of each
mould quickly into hot water and
run a knife around the top edge. Turn
out on to serving plates and decorate
with lime zest and rose petals, if using.

STEP 3

MOULDING THE KULFI

Traditionally this dessert is frozen in
special conical-shaped moulds, but you
can use dariole moulds, small yogurt pots
or fromage frais cartons instead.

STEP 3

SAFFRON-SPICED RICE PUDDING

This rich and comforting pudding is first cooked in milk delicately flavoured with saffron and cinnamon. Raisins, dried apricots, almonds and cream are then added to the mixture before baking.

STEP 1

SERVES 4–5

600 ml/1 pint/2½ cups creamy milk
several pinches of saffron strands, finely
   crushed (see below)
60 g/2 oz/¼ cup short-grain rice
1 cinnamon stick or piece of cassia bark
45 g/1½ oz granulated sugar
30 g/1 oz/¼ cup seedless raisins or
   sultanas
30 g/1 oz/¼ cup ready-soaked dried
   apricots, chopped
1 egg, beaten
75 ml/3 fl oz/5 tbsp single cream
15 g/½ oz/1 tbsp butter, diced
15 g/½ oz/2 tbsp flaked (slivered) almonds
freshly grated nutmeg for sprinkling
cream to serve (optional)

1 Place the milk and crushed saffron in a non-stick saucepan and bring to the boil. Stir in the rice and cinnamon stick, reduce the heat and simmer very gently, uncovered, for 25 minutes, stirring frequently until tender.

2 Remove the pan from the heat and discard the cinnamon stick from the rice mixture. Stir in the sugar, raisins and apricots, then beat in the egg, cream and diced butter.

3 Transfer the mixture to a greased ovenproof pie or flan dish, sprinkle with the almonds and freshly grated nutmeg, to taste. Cook in a preheated oven at 160°C/325°F/Gas Mark 3 for 25–30 minutes until the mixture is set and lightly golden. Serve hot with extra cream, if wished.

STEP 2

STEP 2

SAFFRON

For a slightly stronger saffron flavour, place the saffron strands on a small piece of kitchen foil and toast them lightly under a hot grill for a few moments (take care not to overcook them or the flavour will spoil) and crush finely between fingers and thumb before adding to the milk.

STEP 3

STEP 1

STEP 2

STEP 3

STEP 3

COCONUT CREAM MOULDS

Smooth, creamy and refreshing – these tempting little custards are made with an unusual combination of coconut milk, cream and eggs.

SERVES 8

CARAMEL:
125 g/4 oz/¹/₂ cup granulated sugar
150 ml/¹/₄ pint/²/₃ cup water

CUSTARD:
300 ml/¹/₂ pint/1¹/₄ cups water
90g/3 oz creamed coconut, chopped
2 eggs
2 egg yolks
1¹/₂ tbsp caster sugar
300 ml/¹/₂ pint/1¹/₄ cups single (light) cream
1–2 tbsp freshly grated or desiccated (shredded) coconut

1 Have ready 8 small ovenproof dishes about 150 ml/¹/₄ pint/²/₃ cup capacity. To make the caramel, place the sugar and water in a saucepan and heat gently to dissolve the sugar, then boil rapidly, without stirring, until the mixture turns a rich golden brown.

2 Remove at once from the heat and dip the base of the pan into a basin of cold water (this stops it cooking). Quickly but carefully pour the caramel into the ovenproof dishes to coat the bases.

3 To make the custard, place the water in the same saucepan, add the coconut and heat until the coconut dissolves, stirring all the time. Place the eggs, egg yolks and caster sugar in a bowl and beat well with a fork. Add the hot coconut milk and stir well to dissolve the sugar. Stir in the cream and strain the mixture into a jug.

4 Arrange the dishes in a roasting tin (pan) and fill the tin (pan) with enough cold water to come halfway up the sides of the dishes. Pour the custard mixture into the caramel-lined dishes, cover with baking parchment or foil and cook in a preheated oven at 140°C/275°F/Gas Mark 1 for about 40 minutes or until set.

5 Remove the dishes from the roasting tin (pan) and leave to cool. Chill overnight in the refrigerator. To serve, run a knife around the edge of each dish and turn out on to a serving plate. Serve sprinkled with freshly grated or desiccated (shredded) coconut.

STEP 1

STEP 2

STEP 3

STEP 4

LASSI YOGURT DRINK

This is a deliciously fragrant drink that you can easily imagine the maharajas' ladies sipping! The choice of the sweet or savoury version is entirely a matter of taste.

SERVES 4

SWEET VERSION:
600 ml/ 1 pint/ 2½ cups natural yogurt
600 ml/ 1 pint/ 2½ cups water
1 tsp rosewater
4 tsp caster (superfine) sugar
4 cardamom pods, crushed, pods discarded
1 tbsp pistachio nuts

SAVOURY VERSION:
600 ml/ 1 pint/ 2½ cups natural yogurt
600 ml/ 1 pint/ 2½ cups water
¼ tsp salt
1 tsp sugar
¼ tsp cumin seeds, ground and roasted
sprigs of fresh mint to garnish

1 For both versions, put the yogurt and water in a bowl or jug and whisk together until smooth.

2 For the sweet version, stir in the rosewater, caster sugar and cardamom pods. Add more sugar if required. Mix together well.

3 Chop the pistachio nuts. Serve over ice and decorate with chopped pistachios.

4 For the savoury version, stir the salt, sugar and cumin into the yogurt and water.

5 Mix together well, serve over ice and garnish with mint sprigs.

ROSEWATER

Rosewater has acquired very romantic connotations, not least because it was precious enough to be offered up to the gods in times past. It is made from the extracts of rose petals, and is not too expensive to buy in small quantities. It is available from good supermarkets, health food stores and delicatessens.

Indian Cuisine

INDIAN CUISINE

Here is a selection of easy
accompaniments to serve with
Indian meals.

Apple & Onion Relish
Peel and core 1 large cooking
apple and coarsely grate into a
bowl. Add a bunch of chopped
spring onions (scallions), 2 tsp
vinegar or lemon juice, 1–2 tsp
caster (superfine) sugar and
roasted cumin seeds. Stir well,
then cover and chill before
serving, garnished with
chopped fresh coriander
(cilantro).

Radish & Cucumber Yogurt
Put 600 ml/1 pint/2½ cups
natural yogurt in a bowl and
season with salt and pepper.
Stir in ½ bunch trimmed and
coarsely chopped radishes,
¼ unpeeled, diced cucumber, 1
small chopped onion and 1–2
tbsp chopped fresh mint. Cover
and chill before serving.

Carrot, Raisin & Onion Salad
Coarsely grate 1 large carrot
into a bowl. Add 1 very thinly
sliced onion, 3 tbsp seedless
raisins and 1 tbsp lemon juice.
Season with ¼ tsp paprika,
½ tsp grated fresh ginger, salt
and pepper. Stir well and leave
to stand for 20 minutes so the
flavours develop before
serving. For extra flavour, stir
in finely chopped fresh dill.

With India's vast geographical range and
varied natural resources, cooking is
highly regional. In the past, difficult
transportation meant that cooks could
not obtain fresh ingredients from other
parts of the country, so local dishes
developed, making the most of available
produce. The number of religions
throughout India also has a strong
influence on food and cooking, as each
has its own strict dietary code.

The diversity of Indian cuisine is most
obvious in the contrast between the rich,
meat-based dishes served with bread in
the northern states of Punjab, Kashmir
and Uttar Pradesh, and the spicy-hot,
pulse-based vegetarian cuisine of the
south, where rice is the staple
accompaniment.

NORTHERN INDIA
Even today, food from the north reflects
the influence of Muslim Moguls who
conquered India in the sixteenth century.
The invaders brought with them a love of
good living and rich Persian recipes for
fragrant and flavourful rice dishes, such
as the nut and fruit pilaus and the
saffron-flavoured meat and rice
casseroles called biryanis. Mogul courts
located in northern cities became the
sites of lavish banquets and great feasts;
gold and silver platters were piled high
with mounds of subtly flavoured and
beautifully coloured foods, garnished
with thin leaves of pounded silver called
vark. This legacy lives on, in that the
food prepared for today's great

celebrations – weddings, births, family
gatherings – will be mogul-style dishes.

Other popular dishes that reflect the
Mogul influence, both locally and on
Indian restaurant menus aroundthe
world, include kormas – braised meat in
creamy sauces, and koftas – spicy
meatballs that are grilled (broiled) then
slowly cooked in rich sauces. Dishes from
these areas often include the words
mughlai and shahi in their titles.
Mughlai food is spicy and rich, as it is
traditionally cooked in ghee. Cream and
almonds are regular ingredients in these
dishes. The southern city of Hyderabad is
an exception to the north/south divide as
the richness of northern-style Mogul
cooking continues here today.

Punjab is also the home of tandoori
dishes, where marinated meat and
seafood are cooked in clay ovens called
tandoors which are positioned over
charcoal or wood-burning fires. Tandoori
chicken is probably the best-known
tandoori dish, but leavened naan breads
are also cooked on the sides of the oven.
Modern homes rarely include tandoori
ovens, so the grill (broiler) or outdoor
barbecue are more commonly used.
Purists say the results are not the same,
but the food is still dry on the outside and
tender and succulent inside.

Large numbers of Indians living in the
north of the country are Hindus, to
whom the cow is sacred, so beef is rare.
Fragrant long-grain basmati rice, grown
in the foothills of the Himalayas, forms
the basis of the pilaus and biryanis.

SOUTHERN INDIA

Rice is served with every meal in the southern regions of India, and as it doesn't grow there, it has to be transported from the north. Rice is used to absorb the characteristic liquid-style curries and is served with pulse-based dishes to provide protein – vital in an area which is overwhelmingly vegetarian.

In the hot and humid eastern plains that surround Bengal, the mustard plant flourishes, providing oil for cooking and spicy seeds for flavouring. Rice and seafood appear in many meals, often flavoured with mustard oil.

Seafood, coconut and fresh chillies are cooked in endless combinations in the western coastal regions around Goa. This is the home of the ultra-hot vindaloo curries, given a distinctive hot and sour flavour by local chillies and vinegar. Christian communities were established here when the region was conquered by the Portuguese, and their influence means that pork vindaloos are found, unlike areas with large Muslim or Hindu populations. The region is also the home of 'Bombay Duck'. Neither from Bombay nor a duck, it is actually a small fish that is dried in the sun and sold in thin strips.

In hot Madras and the surrounding southern states, highly spiced grains and lentils make up a substantial part of the daily diet, with rice and lentils often combined in a single dish. Meals also include a selection of the lush exotic fruit that thrive in the hot, tropical climate. Bananas are a daily snack, while the trees' large, shiny green leaves are used as serving platters instead of plates.

INDIAN MEALS

Traditionally, all the dishes in an Indian meal are served at once, without any concept of courses. Although Indian restaurants in the West follow our style of serving different courses, this is not the way in typical Indian homes, whether they are vegetarian or meat-eating families. A meal in a meat-eating home will consist of a meat dish, a vegetable dish, a pulse dish, a chutney or relish for accompaniment and, in the south, a large bowl of steaming rice or, in the north, freshly baked bread. Each of the dishes is selected to provide a harmonious blend of flavours. The meal may be served in individual bowls for the diners to help themselves, or each person may have their own thali – a large metal plate with individual bowls on it.

Creamy Indian ice cream (kulfi), a pudding or fresh fruit may be served as a dessert. In the north as well as the south it is customary for Indians to eat with the fingers of the right hand, rather than cutlery, except possibly when entertaining Western guests. Northern diners use just their fingertips or pieces of flat, unleavened bread, such as chapatis, while southerners are quite skilled at using their whole hand. It is not acceptable to use the left hand while eating as it is considered unclean.

Indians have a sweet tooth and like to eat various sweets throughout the day, bought from special stores or on street corners. Many are brightly coloured and all are very sweet, flavoured with coconut, nuts or rose water. Such sweets are an essential part of many religious celebrations.

INDIAN DRINKS

When serving spicy dishes be sure to have plenty of refreshing drinks to hand – chilled mineral water, iced water and fruit juice are ideal. For special occasions and for a deliciously refreshing drink to sip during a hot, spicy meal, serve iced water flavoured with whole spices such as cardamom pods, cumin seeds or cinnamon sticks.

Wine is generally not a good accompaniment to Indian foods as the taste is overpowered by the strong flavours in the food. Instead, serve chilled lagers and beers. For a really authentic drink, serve Lassi (see page 222), the delicious Indian drink of lightly spiced yogurt which is the perfect way to cool the palate.

OPENING A COCONUT

Before you buy a coconut, give it a good shake to make sure you can hear plenty of liquid sloshing around inside; the more liquid it has, the fresher it will be. Use a hammer and screw driver or the tip of a sturdy knife to poke out the three soft 'eyes' in the top, and shake out all the coconut water. Use the hammer to tap the coconut around the centre until it splits in half. Crack the coconut halves into manageable pieces, then break away the shell. Peel off the thin brown skin. You can then grate the white coconut flesh by hand or in a food processor. The grated flesh will freeze for up to three months and can be used straight from frozen in curries and other cooked dishes.

SEEDING CHILLIES

The heat in a chilli comes from a substance in the core and the seeds, so remove these before you chop the chilli if you do not want your dish to be too hot. Cut the chilli in half lengthways and use the tip of the knife to remove the seeds and core. Take care not to touch your face, eyes or mouth until after you have washed your hands or they will sting.

INDIAN INGREDIENTS

It's never been easier to create quick and authentic-tasting Indian food thanks to the marvellous range of exciting spices, tempting ingredients and ready-prepared products so widely available. All the ingredients used in the recipes in this book are easy to find in large supermarkets and Asian grocery stores.

FRESH INGREDIENTS
Chillies

Much of the heat in Indian dishes comes from the use of fresh green chillies, although dried and ground red chillies are also commonplace in Indian kitchens. In southern India, with its searingly hot temperatures, chillies are used in copious amounts because they cause the body to perspire, which has a cooling affect. It's not surprising, therefore, that southern India is home to the fiery hot vindaloo curries. Numerous varieties of fresh chilli grow in India and they come in a range of sizes and intensities, from fairly mild to very hot. As a general rule, the smaller a chilli is, the hotter it will be. Although most recipes specify deseeded chillies, it is really a matter of personal taste, but be warned – the seeds contain most of the heat. Fresh chillies will keep for about five days in the refrigerator.

Coconut

Fresh coconut milk is unmistakable in both savoury and sweet dishes from the area around Goa and in many of the vegetarian dishes of southern India. Coconut milk and the freshly grated flesh are regularly included in rich seafood curries, and the flesh is often added to chutneys for its slightly crunchy texture as well as its flavour. Fresh coconut provides the best flavour but when it isn't available substitute creamed or powdered coconut (see Store-cupboard Ingredients, below.)

Coriander (cilantro)

Although this herb looks like flat-leaf parsley, it has a more pronounced flavour and the two herbs are not interchangeable. Both the leaves and finely chopped stems are used in Indian cooking, to flavour dishes and as edible garnishes. To store fresh coriander (cilantro), put the roots in a glass of water and keep in a cool place for up to four days.

Herbs

Indian cooks use many fresh herbs to balance spicy flavours and to add freshness to dishes. To release their full flavour, fresh herbs should be bruised or chopped before they are combined with other ingredients. Basil, coriander (cilantro), mint and parsley are popular fresh herbs in Indian cooking. If cooking with basil or mint, use only the leaves, although the stalks of parsley and coriander (cilantro) also contain flavour and can be finely chopped and added to simmering curries and other casseroles. When you buy fresh herbs, look for firm stalks and leaves which look like they have 'bounce' in them: limp and yellowing leaves are a sign that the herb is not fresh. To store herbs, rinse off any dirt, then put the stems in a jar of water that comes up to the leaves. They are then best stored in the refrigerator but can also be left at room temperature. Fresh leaves can also be finely chopped and frozen in small containers so they can be used straight from the freezer.

Garlic

Native to India, garlic adds its sharp, distinctive flavour to dishes throughout the country, and is one of the essential ingredients of the rich Mogul dishes from northern India. It is also popular for flavouring vegetarian dishes, when it is often teamed with fresh ginger. Garlic keeps well at room temperature providing the room isn't too warm, in which case it should be stored in the refrigerator.

Ginger

Spicy vegetarian and Mogul dishes often contain ginger for its characteristic flavour and aroma. The gnarled pale brown roots are sold in supermarkets and Asian grocery stores. Peel before use then grate or chop finely. Indian cooks often pound ginger into a paste with onions and other spices, and in Mogul cooking a classic flavouring combination is ginger, garlic and onions, often pounded together. Although ground ginger is a popular ingredient in Western baking recipes, do not substitute it for fresh ginger in savoury Indian recipes.

Yogurt

Rich in protein and calcium, yogurt plays an important part in Indian vegetarian cooking, as well as many meat dishes. It is used as a marinade, as a creamy flavouring in curries and sauces and as a cooling accompaniment to hot dishes. Thick natural yogurt most closely resembles the yogurt made in many Indian homes.

STORE-CUPBOARD INGREDIENTS
Coconut milk and creamed coconut

When fresh coconut isn't available, these two ingredients are ideal for adding an authentic Indian flavour to sweet and savoury dishes. Coconut milk is sold in cans or in powdered form that has to be made up with water. Creamed coconut is sold in compressed bars and can be added directly to dishes or reconstituted first with water. It gives a richer flavour and texture than canned or powdered coconut milk. You can make coconut milk by soaking unsweetened desiccated (shredded) coconut in water and then straining it through muslin (cheesecloth) and squeezing out all the flavoured liquid. Do not confuse creamed coconut with coconut cream, which is a very sweet, thick, syrup-like mixture used in cocktails.

Ghee

Many Indian recipes specify using ghee as the cooking fat. This is because it is similar to clarified butter in that it can be heated to a very high temperature without burning. Ghee adds a nutty flavour to dishes and a glossy shine to sauces. You can buy ghee in cans, and a vegetarian version is also available. Store at room temperature or keep in the refrigerator. If it is not available, substitute a mixture of sunflower oil and butter – the oil prevents the butter from burning when heated.

COOKING BASMATI RICE

This is a foolproof way to cook long-grain rice by the absorption method. Do not be tempted to lift the lid before the time is up, or the steam will escape and the rice will not cook properly.

250 g/8 oz/1¼ cups basmati rice

Put the rice in a fine sieve (strainer) and rinse under cold running water until the water runs clear. Put the rice in a bowl, cover with fresh water and leave to soak for 30 minutes. Drain off the water. Place the rice in a heavy-based saucepan and add enough water so the water level is 2.5 cm/1 inch above the rice.
  Place the pan over a high heat and bring to the boil, then stir well. Cover the pan tightly, turn off the heat and leave for 25 minutes. Remove the pan from the burner and leave to stand for a further 10 minutes before removing the lid. Fluff up the rice with a fork and serve.

COOKING WITH SPICES

Indian cooks use several techniques to coax all the flavour out of dried spices and give dishes well harmonized flavours that do not taste raw.

The first technique is to dry fry or roast whole seeds over a gentle heat. As the spices roast, they begin to jump around in the pan, so it is a good idea to use a heavy-based frying pan (skillet) with a lid. Dry frying takes only a few minutes and you will be able to tell when the spices are ready because of the wonderful fragrance that develops. Be sure to stir the spices constantly and never take your eyes off the pan because the spices can burn very quickly. See page 231 for a recipe for a Dry Fried Spice Mix prepared this way.

The second technique is to slowly fry the spices in the ghee or vegetable oil that will be used for cooking the other ingredients. This has the advantage of not only bringing out the flavours of the spices, but also adding spiciness to the cooking oil.

Gram flour

Also called besan flour, this pale yellow flour is made from ground chick-peas (garbanzo beans). In Indian kitchens it is used to make breads, bhajis and batters and to thicken sauces and stabilize yogurt when it is added to hot dishes. Buy it from Indian food stores or large health food stores and store in a cool, dark place in an air-tight container.

Dried herbs

Dried, freeze-dried and frozen herbs are great stand-bys when fresh ones aren't available. You can extract extra flavour from dried herbs if you warm them in the oven before you use them. Just spread them out on a baking sheet (cookie sheet) and place in a preheated low oven for 3–4 minutes until they become fragrant. You will be able to smell the aroma when they are ready.

Nuts

Pale green pistachios, cashews and almonds are regular ingredients in both savoury and sweet Indian cooking. The nuts are used both whole and finely ground, when they are often used to thicken sauces. It is best to buy whole nuts and grind them yourself, rather than using packets of ready-ground nuts. Freshly ground nuts have the best flavour as grinding releases their natural oils.

Cooking oils

Indian cooks use a variety of vegetable oils, and groundnut or sunflower oil make good alternatives for most dishes, although sometimes more specialist ones are called for:

Coconut oil Particularly popular in southern and western India, this oil is extracted from coconut flesh and has a mild taste.

Mustard oil In Bengal, cooks favour this dark golden oil with a pungent flavour. It is also used in pickles throughout India.

Sesame oil Unlike Chinese sesame oil, the Indian variety is light and colourless. Spices are often fried in it before being combined with other ingredients.

Pulses

Dried beans, peas and lentils are an essential ingredient in the Indian kitchen, especially in vegetarian homes where, combined with a grain dish and a dairy product, they provide one of the main sources of protein. Indian cooking is renowned for its interesting and delicious range of pulse dishes, usually known as dal.

When you buy dried pulses, always check the package for any small stones or husks that should be removed before you cook them. Dried pulses keep for up to six months in an air-tight container, after which the skins begin to toughen, so buy your pulses from a store with a fast turnover. Do not season pulses until after cooking as the salt may also cause them to become tough. Never overlook the option of using canned pulses, which simply have to be drained and rinsed before use. As canned beans and peas tend to be quite soft in texture, they are usually added to dishes towards the end of the cooking time to prevent them becoming too soft. Here is a list of the pulses that are most frequently used in Indian cooking:

Black-eyed beans These oval-shaped beans are grey or beige with a dark dot in the centre. They have a slightly smoky flavour. They are sold canned as well as dried.

Chana dal Similar to yellow split peas in appearance, they are husked and split black chick-peas (garbanzo beans). The flavour is slightly sweeter than that of yellow split peas and the grains are smaller. You will also see these sold as channa dal.

Chick-peas (garbanzo beans) Cream coloured and resembling a hazelnut in appearance, these peas have a nutty flavour and slightly crunchy texture. Indian cooks also grind these to make a flour called gram or besan, which is used to make breads, to thicken sauces, and to make batters for deep-fried dishes such as onion bhajis.

Lentils As well as the familiar green-brown variety of lentils, Indians also cook a great deal with split red and yellow lentils, which have milder flavours. All varieties have the advantage of not needing pre-soaking or boiling before cooking, which makes them the most convenient pulses to use. Be careful, however, not to over-cook lentils or their texture will be reduced to a pulpy mess.

Red kidney beans Popular to use in spicy stews, soups and sauces, these beans have a nutty flavour and are readily available canned. If using dried ones, don't forget to boil them hard for 10 minutes before simmering. This is essential to kill a poisonous enzyme they contain. Canned red kidney beans, however, do not need boiling.

Rice

Long grain rice is an important ingredient in Indian cooking, especially for vegetarians and in southern India where bread is rarely served. Basmati rice, grown in the Himalayan foothills, has long, slender grains with a delicate flavour that sets it apart from other long-grain rices and accounts for its higher price. You can substitute American or Patna long-grain rice for basmati, but the result will not be quite as good. Easy-cook and brown versions of basmati rice are sold in supermarkets.

Rose water

The diluted essence extracted from rose petals is a popular ingredient in Indian desserts, and an essential flavouring of many Mogul dishes. It adds an exotic quality to drinks and sweetmeats. You can buy it in delicatessens, supermarkets and Indian food stores. Only a few drops are needed to flavour a dish.

Spices

Spices play an essential part in Indian cooking but don't let the vast array on supermarket shelves put you off. You will only need a few familiar spices to give your cooking an authentic taste. It is best to buy whole spices and grind them as needed because they keep their flavour and aroma much longer than ready-ground spices. You can grind spices in a pestle and mortar or use a spice grinder or small electric food processor that you keep just for that purpose. Buy your spices in small quantities and store them in a cool, dark place so they stay fresh and retain their aroma. If you do buy

DRY-FRIED SPICE MIX

The simple technique of dry-frying mellows the flavours of seeds and spices. All you need is a frying pan (skillet) to make this handy spice mixture. Be sure to watch the seeds and stir constantly while they are browning because they can burn very quickly. Add 1 teaspoon to rice, pulses or stews during cooking to give an authentic flavour. It will keep in an airtight container for up to one month.

4 tbsp coriander seeds
1 tbsp cumin seeds

Heat a small frying pan (skillet) over a medium heat. When it is hot, add the coriander and cumin seeds and fry, stirring constantly, until they turn a few shades darker. You should be able to smell the aroma from the seeds.

Immediately pour the seeds out of the pan on to a plate and leave them to cool.

Using a pestle and mortar or a small electric spice grinder, grind the seeds as finely as possible.

GARAM MASALA

You can buy this traditional blend of spices ready-made, or you can make your own.

2 tbsp cumin seeds
2 tbsp coriander seeds
1 tbsp black peppercorns
2 tsp cloves
1 tsp cardamom seeds
2 dried bay leaves
1 cinnamon stick, about 7.5
*   cm/ 3 inches*
1 dried red chilli

Place all the ingredients in a pestle and mortar , small food processor or spice grinder and process until finely ground. Store in an air-tight container.

ground spices, however, be sure to check that they are not past the sell-by date as the flavour and fragrance will probably have deteriorated. Here are the most common spices used in Indian dishes:

Ajowan Related to caraway and cumin, these small brown seeds are valued for their digestive properties. They are used in vegetable dishes, especially in southern India, and in breads.

Aniseed Similar to fennel seeds, these small seeds are a popular ingredient in food from the Bengali and Kashmiri regions. They taste and smell similar to liquorice. They are also available ground from Indian food stores.

Cardamom These small pods contain numerous tiny black seeds which have a warm flavour and are highly aromatic – green cardamoms are considered the best because of their fine, delicate flavour. Black pods make an adequate substitute, but they have a much stronger flavor. Green cardamoms are also prized for their digestive properties, and some Indians chew them raw after they have eaten extra-spicy curries, to aid digestion and sweeten the breath. Used in both sweet and savoury dishes, cardamom pods are usually lightly crushed prior to use to allow the full flavour of the seeds to be appreciated. Whole or crushed cardamom pods are not meant to be eaten, so they should be removed before serving or left on the side of the plate. Some recipes specify using just the seeds rather than the whole pod. To remove the seeds, use the end of a rolling pin or a pestle and mortar to break open the pod and take out the seeds. Ground cardamom is the finely ground pods.

Cassia This spice comes from the bark of the cassia tree. It is similar in appearance and flavour to cinnamon but is not as uniform in shape. Cinnamon can be used in its place.

Chilli The quickest way to add heat to a curry or other Indian dish is to add a crumbled dried red chilli, or dried chilli flakes. For extra heat add the seeds as well. Ground chillies are sold as chilli powder or cayenne pepper.

Cinnamon Shavings of bark from the cinnamon tree are processed and curled to form the sticks of this fragrant spice. The sticks are not edible, although they make an attractive garnish as well as adding flavour to sweet and savoury dishes. Cinnamon is also available ground.

Cloves These dried, unopened flower buds are used to give flavour and aroma to both sweet and savoury dishes, but should be used with caution because the flavour can be overwhelming if too many are used. Whole cloves are not meant to be eaten. Cloves are one of the spices traditionally included in garam masala.

Coriander Available ground or as seeds, this spice is one of the essential ingredients in Indian cooking. Coriander seeds are often dry roasted before use to develop their flavour.

Cumin These caraway-like seeds are popular with Indian cooks because of their warm, pungent flavour and aroma. The seeds are sold whole or ground, and are usually included as one of the flavourings in garam masala.

Fenugreek The seed of this herb is used for its bitter flavour and pronounced aroma, especially in vegetarian dishes and pickles. You will find the seeds and a ground version in Indian grocery stores.

Garam Masala This is actually a mixture of ground spices, not an individual spice. The usual combination includes cardamom, cinnamon, cloves, cumin, nutmeg and black peppercorns, but most Indian cooks have a personal recipe, often handed down for generations. Garam masala is usually added to savoury dishes at the end of cooking so the heat doesn't destroy the subtle flavouring. You can buy prepared garam masala at large supermarkets or Asian grocery stores or make your own (see page 232).

Mustard seeds These tiny, reddish-brown seeds are used throughout India, and are a particularly important ingredient in pickles and in southern vegetarian cooking. The leaves and oil are also included in many dishes. Mustard seeds are often fried in oil or ghee to bring out their flavour before being combined with other ingredients. You can substitute the black seeds more commonly found in Western supermarkets.

Onion seeds Always used whole in Indian cooking, these tiny black seeds are used in pickles and often sprinkled over the top of naan breads. Ironically, onion seeds don't have anything to do with the vegetable, but they look similar to the plant's seed, hence the name.

Paprika Used for colouring dishes as well as flavouring them, this bright red-orange spice is similar to chilli powder but has a much milder flavour.

Poppy seeds In India, poppy seeds are white, not black, and used for their thickening properties. Look for white seeds in Indian food stores and some health food stores; do not substitute black poppy seeds as the flavour is very different.

Saffron The most expensive of all spices, saffron strands are the stamens of a type of crocus. They give dishes a rich, golden colour, as well as adding a distinctive, slightly bitter taste. Some books recommend substituting turmeric for saffron, but although the colours are similar, the tastes are not. Saffron is sold as a powder or in strands. Saffron strands are more expensive but do have a superior flavour.

Tamarind Vegetable dishes are often given a sharp, sour flavour with the inclusion of tamarind juice. This is made from the semi-dried, compressed pulp of the tamarind tree. You can buy bars of the pungent-smelling pulp in Indian and oriental grocery stores. Store it in a tightly sealed plastic bag or air-tight container.

Turmeric This aromatic root is dried and ground to produce the distinctive bright yellow-orange powder used in many Indian dishes. It has a warm, aromatic smell and a full, somewhat musty taste.

COOKING EQUIPMENT

Although Indian cooks are masters of delicious, exotic food, their kitchens are not very differently equipped than those found in Western homes. You won't have to make any major investments in specialist equipment to create authentic-tasting meals.

A large, deep pan similar to a wok and several heavy-based saucepans or flameproof casseroles are the most

STABILIZING YOGURT

Yogurt is often used in Indian dishes but great care has to be taken so that it doesn't overheat and curdle. To prevent this happening you can stir in the yogurt a spoonful at a time at the end of cooking, making sure each spoonful is fully incorporated before the next is added. Or you can blend the yogurt with a little cornflour (cornstarch) or gram flour ($\frac{1}{2}$ tsp for every 150 ml/$\frac{1}{4}$ pint/$\frac{2}{3}$ cup) before adding it to the dish.

QUICK-COOKING PULSES

All whole, dry pulses, apart from lentils, should be soaked overnight before cooking, or use this quick-cook method.

Place the pulses in a pan, cover with water, bring to the boil and boil for 10 minutes. Remove from the heat, cover and leave to soak for 3 hours. Drain and place the pulses in a clean pan, cover with fresh water and bring to the boil. Boil hard for 10 minutes, then simmer for the amount of time specified in the recipe.

This second boiling is important to kill poisonous toxins present in some pulses. Don't forget that the total cooking time will depend on the freshness of the pulses: the fresher they are, the quicker they will cook.

important pieces of equipment, as most Indian cooking is done on top of the stove. In fact, Indians don't use anything that is the equivalent of a Western stove. The traditional Indian oven, called a tandoor, was made of clay and built into the ground, but it is more a feature of restaurant cooking today and very few homes have one. In rural areas, cooking is done on a basic coal- or wood-burning stove built near the floor in the corner of the kitchen. The cook squats in front of the stove or sits on a low stool next to it.

Here is a guide to the everyday pieces of equipment needed to produce authentic Indian meals.

Blender

Use a blender to quickly mix cooling drinks, such as the yogurt-based lassi. As an alternative, put all the ingredients in a bowl and use a whisk to blend them.

Degchi

This handleless pan is made of aluminium or brass, has a tight-fitting lid and is similar to the traditional French daubiere. Used for cooking slowly braised dishes, its lid is designed to hold hot coals so ingredients are gently cooked by heat from the top as well as the bottom. A heavy-based flameproof casserole will produce similar results.

Food processor

Although not essential, modern Indian cooks find using one of these is the most efficient way to cope with all the chopping involved in Indian cooking. It is also useful for chopping large amounts of fresh herbs and making pastes from garlic, ginger and onions. A small food processor, or coffee grinder, is ideal for grinding spices. If you choose this option instead of using a pestle and mortar, however, remember to use it exclusively for grinding spices as it will flavour any other foods put in there.

Frying pan (skillet)

A non-stick frying pan (skillet) is useful for dry-frying seeds and spices to bring out their flavours before they are ground.

Karhai

This is an Indian version of the versatile Chinese wok. It is used for deep-frying or for slowly simmered meat, poultry, seafood and pulse dishes. Many Indian homes have two karhais, a deep one with a narrow top which is used for deep frying, and a shallower one with a much wider top which is used for occasional stir-frying and simmering. Like a wok it is the curved sides that make this such a useful piece of equipment, because the sides provide a much larger cooking surface than a conventional frying pan (skillet) or saucepan. A traditional Chinese wok is a suitable substitute. Woks come in numerous sizes and are made of various materials, such as cast iron, aluminium, stainless-steel and even brass. You can also buy woks with non-stick finishes, which are particularly useful if you want to reduce the amount of fat in some recipes. When you buy a wok, look for one with one long wooden handle or two wooden handles on the sides so you can grip it without burning your hands. Some woks, especially those made of cast iron, are very heavy, so it is a good idea to pick one up to make sure you can handle it easily. Most woks need a ring that sits over the burner to keep the wok steady while you cook.

Knives

Indian cooking can involve a great deal of chopping, so firm knives with a sharp blade are invaluable. A medium-sized all-purpose knife, called a cook's or kitchen knife, is ideal for most chores, but a flexible, thin-bladed filleting knife is best for filleting fish and a rigid boning knife is what you use for removing meat and poultry bones. Carbon steel can be sharpened very finely, but stainless steel is the usual choice for kitchen knives because it is so easy to take care of. Unlike carbon steel, it doesn't have to be kept dry to prevent it from rusting.

Pestle and mortar

It is easy to buy ground spices and prepared spice mixtures in supermarkets but the flavour of freshly ground spices is vastly superior. A heavy pestle and mortar is useful if you want to grind your own spices. A good-quality set will have a slightly rough surface on the interior of the mortar and on the end of the pestle. They may be made from vitrified porcelain, unglazed porcelain, stone, wood, marble or even heavy-duty glass.

Saucepans

Several medium saucepans with heavy bases are useful for cooking pulses and rice and vegetable dishes. The heavy base is important because it helps to distribute heat evenly, and also retains heat once the pan is taken off the heat. Pans with tight-fitting lids mean they can double as casseroles for cooking on top of the stove, which is useful when you are cooking some of the rice recipes, such pilaus and biryanis. Various materials are used in the manufacture of saucepans and it is a matter of personal choice which you use. Stainless steel is a popular choice because it is hard wearing and easy to clean, but on its own it is not a good conductor of heat. If you want a stainless-steel pan, buy one made of heavy-gauge stainless steel or one with copper or aluminium in the base.

Skewers

A supply of stainless steel or bamboo skewers are useful for barbecuing spicy kebabs and some tandoori recipes. Bamboo skewers should be soaked in water for about 30 minutes before use, to prevent them burning. When you buy stainless steel skewers, choose flat, rather than round ones as these hold the ingredients in place when you turn the skewer. If you rub the skewer with vegetable oil before you put any food on it, the cooked food will come off easily.

Tava

This is the traditional flat griddle used for cooking some Indian breads. A large frying pan (skillet) makes an adequate substitute.

Thali

A large metal, rimmed plate that comes with several metal bowls, called *katoris*. Use thalis if you want to serve your

A karhai or wok made from cast iron needs to be well seasoned with oil to prevent food sticking while it is being cooked, especially if you are shallow frying or stir frying.

Before you use it for the first time, rub a thin layer of vegetable oil over the base and up the sides, then sprinkle thickly with sea salt. Place over a high heat until very hot. Remove from the heat and use a thick wad of crumpled paper towels to wipe the surface clean. Take care not to burn your fingers.

Avoid washing the pan after use if at all possible; simply wipe clean with paper towels, or rinse with water and dry thoroughly. If you have to wash the pan, it must be seasoned again.

COOKING POPPADOMS

Supermarkets and Indian food stores sell packets of these crispy, thin wafers that are so delicious to munch with drinks before an Indian-style meal. Serve them warm with chutneys and relishes for dipping.

To pan fry poppadums, heat about 1 cm/$\frac{1}{2}$ inch vegetable oil in a frying pan (skillet) over a medium heat. The oil should be hot enough for a cube of bread to sizzle instantly when it is dropped in. Use tongs to lower a poppadom into the oil and cook for just a few seconds until it expands and becomes puffy. If it turns dark brown, the oil is too hot.

To grill (broil) poppadoms, brush them with melted ghee or vegetable oil and place under a preheated grill (broiler) for just a few seconds. Use tongs to turn over and continue grilling (broiling) for just a few seconds longer. They should be just lightly speckled with brown.

Indian meal in the authentic way. Each person has their own thali, with a portion of each dish in each bowl. Made of aluminium or brass (sometimes silver or even gold), you can buy thalis from large Asian grocery stores.

Tongs

A pair of long-handled tongs are essential for lifting sizzling food from hot fat when you are deep-frying, or for turning ingredients under a hot grill (broiler).

COOKING METHODS

'Curry' has become a universal euphemism for Indian cooking and food, but although a dish called a curry does exist, this single word does not do justice to the richly varied dishes and cooking styles of the Indian sub-continent.

The word 'curry' is simply a Western way of pronouncing *kari*, a southern Tamil word for sauce or the fragrant leaves of a kari tree. These dried leaves are a main ingredient in a spice mixture called *kari podi*, which has become known as curry powder. Authentic curries are slowly cooked and never include a marinade, yogurt or cream like other spicy dishes do. Because the cooking process is so slow and gentle, meat curries are usually made from older meat, such as mutton, or the tougher cuts. When vegetables, such a peas or potatoes, are included in a meat curry, they are usually added towards the end of the cooking time.

A significant difference between Indian and Western cooking styles is that meat is always trimmed of excess fat and skin is removed from chicken before cooking.

Barbecuing

Before modern kitchens were installed, much of the cooking in India was done over coal or wood fires, and barbecued food remains a favourite. Tandoori chicken, marinated in yogurt and spices which give its glorious reddish-brown colour, is a popular dish for barbecuing, as are all forms of kebabs.

Marinating

This is a technique widely used to add flavour and tenderize less expensive cuts of meat and seafood before they are baked or grilled (broiled), or cooked in a traditional tandoor oven. Sometimes the ingredients are cut into small pieces and submerged in a marinade, while in other recipes the marinade is brushed on to whole fish or chicken breasts. Heavily spiced yogurt is a popular marinade, especially for ingredients that are cooked over charcoal, under a grill (broiler) or in a tandoor. The yogurt turns into a thin crust as it cooks, protecting the flesh beneath. Lemon and lime juices are also used for marinating, as well as paw-paw (papaya), which has a tenderizing effect.

INDIAN MENUS

The names of Indian cooking techniques are often incorporated into recipe titles on menus. These are some of the ones you are most likely to come across:

Bharta

This term describes puréed vegetables. Aubergines (eggplant) are often prepared in this way, first being cooked over a charcoal or wood fire so they develop a smoky flavour.

Bhaghar

This is a simple technique which adds richness and flavour to meat, fish, vegetable, and especially pulse dishes, and counteracts bland flavours. Ghee or vegetable oil is heated in a heavy-based frying pan (skillet), then whole spices and seeds are added and fried until they are golden brown and sizzling. The contents of the pan are poured over the dish a few minutes before serving. The dish is kept covered until ready to serve, to keep in all the aromas.

Bhoona

Also known as brown frying, this technique involves stir-frying onions, garlic, ginger and spices until they turn golden brown. Meat and poultry dishes with reddish-brown sauces often begin with this process and it is an important technique in preparing the classic Mogul dishes of northern India. When chopped or sliced onions are prepared this way they are slowly cooked in ghee, or a vegetable oil, until they turn golden, then the spices are stirred in and the stir-frying continues until the onions lose all their moisture and turn a dark, rich brown. Sukka bhoona in a title indicates that the dish has been sautéed, and this style of dish is usually made with the best, most tender cuts of meat.

Do pyaza

A slowly braised dish combining both cooked and raw onions. The main ingredient, usually meat, is gently cooked with half the onions until very tender, then a second batch of raw onions is stirred in towards the end of cooking to give extra texture and taste. Traditional recipes use 900 g/2 lb onions for each 450 g/1 lb meat. You will also see this dish spelled as dopiaza.

Dum

Similar to pot-roasting, this is the Indian method of cooking ingredients in a tightly sealed container on top of the stove. Traditionally, a pan called a degchi is used, set over hot ashes and with hot coals in its lid. A flameproof casserole can be used, as long as it can be tightly sealed. One method of sealing a container is to make a simple flour and water dough, form it into a roll, place it around the rim and press down the lid. Alternatively, put a large piece of foil under the lid and scrunch the over-hanging foil around the sides.

Korma

These are slowly braised dishes, many of which are the rich and spicy, Persian-inspired Mogul dishes served on special occasions. Yogurt is often featured, both as a marinade and as the cooking liquid. In a properly cooked korma, prime, tender cuts of meat are used, and the small amount of cooking liquid is absorbed back into the meat to produce a succulent result. A heavy-based cooking container with a tight-fitting lid is essential for a korma.

Talawa

This refers to meat, seafood, poultry or vegetables that are coated in crumbs or a batter and deep-fried until golden on the outside and tender in the centre. You will also see these dishes referred to as talana.

VARK

This is edible silver that is used to decorate elaborate dishes prepared for the most special occasions and celebrations, such as weddings. It is pure silver that has been beaten until it is wafer thin. It comes with a piece of backing paper which is peeled off as the vark is laid on the cooked food. It is extremely delicate and so must be handled with care. You can buy vark in Indian food stores, and remember that because it is pure silver it should be stored in an air-tight bag or box so it doesn't tarnish.

INDEX